INSTANT POT COOKBOOK

The Essential Electric Pressure Cooker Recipes Cookbook with Delicious & Healthy Meals for Smart People

(Electric Pressure Cooker Cookbook)

(Instant Pot Cookbook)

BY

Michael Francis

ISBN: 978-1-952504-53-2

COPYRIGHT © 2020 by Michael Francis

All rights reserved. This book is copyright protected and it's for personal use only. Without the prior written permission of the publisher, no part of this publication should be reproduced, distributed, or transmitted in any form or by any means, including photocopying, recording, or other electronic or mechanical methods.

This publication is sold with the idea that the publisher is not required to render accounting, officially permitted, or otherwise, qualified services. If advice is required, it is necessary to seek the services of a legal or professional, a practiced individual in the profession. This document is geared towards providing substantial and reliable information in regards to the topics covered.

DISCLAIMER

The information written in this book is for educational and entertainment purposes only. Strenuous efforts have been made to provide accurate, up to date and reliable complete information. The information in this book is true and complete to the best of our knowledge. All recommendations are made without guarantee on the part of the author and publisher.

Neither the publisher nor the author takes any responsibility for any possible consequences of reading or enjoying the recipes in this book. The author and publisher disclaim any liability in connection with the use of information contained in this book. Under no circumstance will any legal responsibility or blame be apportioned against the author or publisher for any reparation, damages, or monetary loss due to the information herein, either directly or indirectly.

Table of Contents

INTRODUCTION 8
What is an Instant Pot? 9
What are the Benefits of Using an Instant Pot? 10
Making Sense of Those Buttons 12
How your Instant Pot Works 15
Great Tips & Trick for Using Your Instant Pot 16
Instant Pot Must-Have Accessories 18
Cleaning Tips for Your Instant Pot 20
Frequently Asked Questions – FAQ 22
    Before Purchasing Your Instant Pot 22
    After Purchasing Your Instant Pot 23

BREAKFAST 24
    Banana Walnut Steel Cut Oats 24
    Mexican Egg Casserole 25
    Bacon Ranch Potatoes 26
    Vanilla Latte Steel Cut Oats 27
    French Toast Casserole 28
    Buckwheat Porridge 29
    Jamaican Cornmeal Porridge 30
    Breakfast Burrito Casserole 31
    Green Chile Breakfast Tacos 32
    Vanilla Apple Cinnamon Breakfast Quinoa 33
    Spiced Pumpkin Apple Butter 34
    Breakfast Quinoa 35

SOUPS & STEWS 36
    Red Pepper Tomato Soup 36
    Italian Sausage Stew 38
    Chicken Tortilla Soup 40

Spanish Infused Chicken Stew 41

Butternut Cauliflower Soup 42

Beef Lentil Stew 43

Stuffed Pepper Soup 44

Andouille Sausage Stew 45

Cheeseburger Soup 46

Beef & Butternut Squash Stew 47

Hearty Broccoli Soup 49

Spicy Ethiopian Stew 51

POULTRY 52

Chicken Faux Pho 52

Mexican Chicken Soup 54

Orange Chicken 55

Teriyaki Turkey Meatballs 57

Chicken Paprika Stew 59

Honey Lemon Chicken 61

Ground Turkey Lentil Chili 63

BEEF & PORK 64

Beef Masala Curry 64

Pork Vindaloo 66

Spicy Beef Stew 68

Cuban Pulled Pork 69

Beef Luau Stew 71

Mexican Pulled Pork 72

Beef Stroganoff 73

Pork Carnitas 74

Beef and Broccoli 76

Hawaiian Pineapple Pork 78

Boneless Pork Chops 80

Beef Pot Roast 81
FISH & SEAFOODS 83
Creamy Fish Chowder 83
Shrimp Paella 84
Fish Tacos 86
Savory Shrimp with Tomatoes & Feta 87
Shrimp and Lentil Stew 88
Shrimp Coconut Milk 89
Coconut Red Curry Shrimp 90
Crustless Crab Quiche 92
Coconut Fish Curry 94
Salmon with Chili-Lime Sauce 96
Clam Chowder 98
PASTA 100
Cheesy Taco Pasta 100
Cheeseburger Macaroni 101
Chicken Parmesan Casserole 102
Cheesy Chicken & Pasta 104
Vegetable Noodle Soup 105
Chicken, Spinach, and Artichoke Pasta 106
Lasagna Casserole 107
Pizza Pasta 109
Macaroni and Cheese 110
Chicken Fajita Pasta 111
Tuna Noodle Casserole 112
Cauliflower and Pasta Alfredo 113
BEANS, RICE & GRAINS 114
Mexican Green Rice 114
New Orleans-Style Red Beans and Rice 116

13 Bean Soup 117

Baked Beans 118

Red Beans and Rice 119

Rice Pudding 120

Mexican Rice & Beans 121

Pinto Beans & Ham Hocks 122

Spanish Rice with Black Beans and Potatoes 123

Pinto Beans 124

Black Beans 125

VEGAN & VEGETARIAN 126

Cilantro Lime Quinoa 126

Vegan Lentil Chili 127

Quinoa Burrito Bowls 128

Walnut Lentil Tacos 129

Buttery Garlic Mashed Potatoes 131

Mushroom Risotto 132

Lentil Curry 134

Pasta Rigatoni Bolognese 135

Maple Bourbon Sweet Potato Chili 137

Vegan Potato Curry 139

APPETIZERS 140

Beer-Braised Pulled Ham 140

Prosciutto-wrapped Asparagus Canes 141

Buffalo Ranch Chicken Dip 142

Cocktail Meatballs 143

Cranberry Pecan Brie 144

French Apple Cobbler 145

Olive Garden Zuppa Toscana 147

DESSERTS 148

Chocolate Pots De Crème 148

Creamed Corn 149

Chocolate Lava Cake 150

Apple Crisp 151

Homemade Pumpkin Puree 152

Gingerbread Bread Pudding 153

Applesauce 154

ACKNOWLEDGMENT 155

INTRODUCTION

I possess great passion for pressure cooking with my Instant Pot Electric Pressure Cooker. It is a multi-cooker that performs more than seven functions. Instant Pot is a multifunctional fully-programmable Smart cooker combining the benefits of a Pressure Cooker, Slow Cooker, Rice Cooker, Porridge Maker, and Steamer, Sauté pan, Yogurt Maker, Food Warmer and more. It allows you to cook a wide variety of dishes including meat, fish, eggs, grain, poultry, beans, cakes, yogurt and vegetables etc. What makes the Instant Pot exceptional is because you can use different cooking programs such as a steamer, rice cooker, sauté pan, and even a warming pot, thus saving more time, money, and space than buying any other kitchen appliances.

The Instant Pot serves as a multi-use programmable device that can help create easy, fast and delicious recipes with the ability to apply different cooking settings all in one pot. It was developed by clever Canadian technology experts seeking to be the ultimate kitchen devices, from stir-frying, pressure cooking, slow cooking and yogurt and cake making. It was created to serve as a one-stop shop to allow home cooks prepare a flavorful meal with the press of a button. You can cook almost everything in your Instant Pot.

In this book, we will explore the variety of easy delicious dishes you can cook with your Instant Pot. We will explore a wide variety of dishes, from breakfast to dinner, soups to stews, desserts to appetizers, meat to beef, side dishes to vegetables and use a healthy ingredient in the process. The vast majority of the recipes can be prepared and served in less than 45 minutes. Each recipe is written with the exact preparation time, cooking instructions and ingredients required to prepare the dishes. Once you try these delicious dishes with our cookbook, you and your Instant Pot are sure to become inseparable too.

What is an Instant Pot?

An Instant Pot is a multifunctional cooker that acts as a rice cooker, slow cooker, steamer, sauté pan, electric pressure cooker, porridge maker, and a yogurt maker. It is a single kitchen appliance or multi-cooker that does the job of seven different kitchen appliances ranging from electric pressure cooker, rice cooker, steamer, yogurt maker, sauté pan, and warming pot etc. It functions with the combination of steam and pressure which enables your foods to cook quicker and safer than other kitchen devices. It is a programmable countertop multi-cooker which speeds up cooking by 2~6 times using up to 70% less energy.

The Instant Pot can cook nutritious healthy food in a convenient and consistent fashion, making everything from slow-and-low barbecue dishes, stews, rice pilaf, lentil, bacon, chicken and steamed veggies. The Instant Pot deserves a spot in your kitchen because you can rely on it more than any other kitchen devices.

The Instant Pot is a versatile multi-cooker that can execute the function of a pressure cooker, slow cooker, rice cooker, steamer, poultry and more. It has lots of safety features which makes it safer to use and comes in different models. It comes with preset programs that are specifically designed to cook your food to perfection, whether it be a chicken, desserts, cheesecake, a stew, soup, or porridge.

Instant Pot is carefully designed to eliminate many common errors from causing harm or spoiling food. It is manufactured with 10 proven safety mechanisms and patented technologies to protect you from hazards.

What are the Benefits of Using an Instant Pot?

1. **Elimination of Bacteria and Other Micro-Organisms:**

Instant Pots cook your above boiling point, so this will help to eliminate any harmful bacteria, viruses and other toxins that might be lurking in your food. This is especially important in the case of rice, wheat, corn and beans because these foods can harbor substantial amount of toxins, which can make you very sick when consumed. These harmful organisms have even been linked to liver cancer.

2. **Saving Time & Energy:**

The Instant Pot cook foods much faster than any other traditional methods of cooking. Electric pressure cooker can reduce cooking time by up to 70% when compared with any other traditional methods of cooking. Cooking with an Instant Pot requires less water used in cooking and much less energy is required thereby saving up to 70% of energy comparing with boiling, steaming, and slow cooking.

You will save more time and money when cooking with an Instant Pot. An Instant Pot can cook a whole chicken in just half an hour, cook a tender pot roast in less than 2 hours, make a large squash in just 10 minutes and veggies in less than 5 thereby saving more time, energy and money.

3. **Preserving Nutrients & Cook Tasty Food:**

Pressure cooking ensures that heat is evenly and quickly distributed while cooking. The food is not necessarily required to be immersed in water, it simply requires sufficient water to keep the electric pressure cooker filled with steam. The vitamins and minerals will not be dissolved or leached away by water. Because the food is surrounded with the steam, the foods will not be oxidized by air exposure at heat, so asparagus, lentil, broccoli, artichoke, and other veggies retain their bright green colors and phytochemicals. It will also enable the food to retain its original flavor.

Scientific studies have proved that pressure cooking is the best method for retaining the vitamins and minerals of the food that your body needs. Pressure cooking broccoli, for instance, will retain 90% of its vitamin C. The retention when compared to boiling is (66% retention) or steaming (78%). Instant Pot tends to be the healthier option.

4. **Eliminating Harmful Micro-Organisms in Food:**

Foods are pressure cooked at a temperature above the boiling point of water, killing almost all harmful living micro-organisms such as bacteria, fungi, and viruses. It helps to destroy all harmful micro-organisms that are toxic to your health. Some foods such as rice, wheat, corn and beans may carry fungal poisons called aflatoxins.

Aflatoxins are naturally occurring mycotoxins produced by some species of Aspergillus fungi, as a result of improper storage, such as in humid conditions. Research has proved that aflatoxins are a potent trigger of liver cancer and may play a vital role in a host of other cancers too. Aflatoxins cannot be destroyed by just heating your food to the boiling point, they can only be destroyed by pressure cooking.

5. **Helps Boost Digestibility of Foods:**

I believe you must have heard, "You are what you eat." But actually, you are what you absorb from your food. Boosting the digestibility of your food will maximize the nutritional value to your body. Pressure cooking your food makes the toughest meats moist and tender, which is the key to foods that your body can easily digest and absorb.

Making Sense of Those Buttons

Soup:

The Instant Pot has a soup program that is 30 minutes on High Pressure. The Soup feature depends on if you are using fresh or frozen meats. The soup times may range from 20 minutes to an hour. The setting cooks at High Pressure for about 30 minutes. It can be adjusted to more to cook for about 40 minutes. It can also be adjusted to less to cook for about 20 minutes.

2. **Meat / Stew:**

The meat / stew program is 20 minutes on High Pressure. Though, the cooking times may vary depending on the temperature, size, and thickness of the meats. The Meat / Stew function cooks at High Pressure for about 35 minutes. It can be adjusted to more cooks for about 45 minutes and Adjusted to less cooks for about 20 minutes.

3. **Bean / Chili:**

The Bean / Chili program is 30 minutes on High Pressure. The Bean / Chili feature cooks at High Pressure for 30 minutes. It can be adjusted to more cooks for about 40 minutes. The button can also be adjusted to less cooks for about 25 minutes.

4. **Poultry:**

The poultry button is 12 minutes on High Pressure. This cooking time is meant for small portions of uncooked chicken. Larger portions of chicken will require a cooking time of about 25 minutes to reach a center temperature of 165°F. The Poultry function cooks at High Pressure for 15 minutes. The button can be adjusted to more cooks for about 30 minutes and Adjusted to less cooks for about 5 minutes.

5. **Slow Cook:**

The Slow Cook button can be programmed from between 30 minutes to 20 hours and the cooking time can be lowered up to 24 hours. The Slow Cook mode can be set to normal (which is equivalent to low), more (which is equivalent to high), or less (which is equivalent to keep warm mode).

6. **Sauté:**

The sauté button can be used to brown your meat inside your Instant Pot. The temperature of the sauté feature can be adjusted by using the 'Adjust' function to cycle through the modes of less, normal, and more. The temperature mode needs to be adjusted within 10 seconds of pressing the sauté feature. When you press the Sauté function, kindly wait until it displays "Hot" before adding your ingredients into the pot.

7. **Pressure:**

The pressure setting works as a toggle between Low and High-Pressure function. It can simply be used to switch between High and Low-pressure settings for different pressure cooking programs.

8 Manual:

The Manual feature can be used to start pressure cooking. It can be used to switch between low and high pressure by using the 'pressure' function within 10 seconds of pressing the 'Manual' button. You can set a pressure level and cook time using the Adjust and [+] or [-] buttons. When the time is up, the timer will begin to count down.

9 Adjust:

This button can be used to adjust the temperature of the slow cooking and sauté settings between less, normal, and more. This button can be used to toggle from the Less, Normal and More settings. You can select any of the feature you wish to use and press Adjust until the light under Less, Normal and More is adjusted to the desired setting.

10 Timer:

The timer setting is for programmed delayed cooking. The button performs the function for both slow cooking mode and regular pressure cooking mode. This setting must be pressed within 10 seconds of setting your cooking program's time and can be adjusted by pressing the + and – buttons.

11 Keep Warm / Cancel:

The Keep Warm button can be used to set the unit into keep warm mode, and another less turns the unit OFF. This setting helps to turn the Auto Keep Warm function ON and OFF. The Keep Warm function keeps the foods in your cooking pot between 145–172°F. This button can also be used to cancel a function or to turn off the Instant Pot.

12 Yogurt:

This function is not included in the IP-LUX series and is a fully-automated program. This feature can be used to make yogurt. You can press this button and Adjust to More for boiling the milk and use Normal for incubating the yogurt.

13 Steam:

This button cooks at High Pressure for about 10 minutes. It can be Adjusted to more cooks for about 15 minutes and Adjusted to less for about 3 minutes. The Steam function is simply normal High-Pressure mode that can be lowered down to 0 minutes. You can perform a quick release once the cooking time is up. This function is very important when cooking leafy vegetables and prevents them from being overcooked.

14 Porridge:

The Porridge button cooks at High Pressure for 20 minutes. It can be adjusted to more cooks for 30 minutes and Adjusted to less cooks for 15 minutes.

15 Multigrain:

The Multigrain button cooks at High Pressure for about 40 minutes. It can be adjusted to more cooks for 45 minutes and pressure cooking time of about 60 minutes. It can also be adjusted to less cooks for about 20 minutes.

16 Rice:

The Rice button is an automated function that begins at 12 minutes. This button functions at low pressure and can cook white or jasmine rice in about 20 minutes flat. The setting is specifically designed for cooking white rice and the cooking time can be adjusted depending on the quantity of water and rice in the cooking pot.

17 Egg:

The Egg button cooks at High Pressure for about 5 minutes. The button can be adjusted to more cooks for about 6 minutes and Adjusted to less cooks for about 4 minutes.

18 Cake:

The Cake button cooks at High Pressure for about 30 minutes. It can be adjusted to more cooks for about 40 minutes and Adjusted to less cooks for about 25 minutes.

How your Instant Pot Works

The mechanism of Instant Pot is very simple. First, you need to dump all the ingredients for the recipe you are preparing into the bottom of your Instant Pot. Do not fill the Instant Pot with excessive content. Once you are done adding all the ingredients into the, lock the lid and ensure that the valve is in sealing position, turn on the pot and let the magic begin. Adjust the timer to the exact pressure recommended for the recipe. The temperature will begin to build up inside the pot, which creates the steam. As the pot is locked, the steam will build up since there's no room for the steam to escape, the boiling point increase and the hyper steam cause the food to cook quickly.

Great Tips & Trick for Using Your Instant Pot

1. Use at least 1/2 Cup of Liquid When Pressure Cooking:

Pressure Cooker makes use of steam to build pressure that cooks your food faster and easier. The inner pot or liner must contain at least ½ to 1 cup of water to create such pressure. This is the only way to pressurize the unit, and it's a very important tip to always remember when utilizing the pressure cooker function on your Instant Pot.

2. Use Multiple Buttons when Cooking:

Don't think you're needed to just make use of only one button in each cooking session. You may start with the Sauté/Browning function to help brown or caramelize the onions at the beginning of the cooking process, and later make use of the Manual pressure cooking button when it's time to add the vegetable and meat ingredients. When the food has done, you can press the Keep Warm button to keep the food warm until you are ready to serve.

3. Adjust The Temperature:

You don't have to relax once you've selected a cooking function because you have to adjust the temperature when using the Sauté or Slow Cooker functions. This will enable you to get the exact cooking temperature recommended to whatever dish you're making. Some recipes may require a slightly higher temperature, while you may want to turn down the heat on other dishes.

4. Add 10-15 Minutes When Using Pressure:

It takes the Instant Pot about 10 minutes to build the required pressure within the inner liner. So you need to add about 10 to 15 minutes of cooking time whenever you're using the Manual or Pressure button to cook. For example, if your breakfast recipes like Buckwheat Porridge requires 30 minutes cooking time, you'll actually want to input 40 or 45 minutes on your Instant Pot device.

5. Never Open the Instant Pot on Manual or Pressure Mode:

The Instant Pot is a very safe kitchen appliance with lots of safety measures when using the Manual or Pressure setting. When you press one of these buttons, ensure that the pressure valve is turned to sealing position. This will help to seal the pressure inside the Instant Pot while you pressure cook. After the mode is selected, you only have 10 seconds to press the Cancel button to stop the cooking process.

6. Change the Inner Pot:

The Instant Pot has an inner liner that can be used to cook your food, although many Instant Pot users love to have multiple inner liners at their disposal. The inner liner enables you to multiple dishes in one cooking session and makes for easier storage too.

Instant Pot accessories, such as steaming racks and silicone molds can also help you cook a wide range of different dishes at the same time in your Instant Pot.

7. Buy Extra Sealing Rings:

You should endeavor to buy a set of extra sealing rings because the sealing rings has a tendency to retain smells of your previously cooked dishes. You can keep one ring for savory dishes and one ring for sweet dishes.

8. Be Careful with Dairy:

The Instant Pot button has a yogurt-making function for making dairy dishes. The function button doesn't always cook creamy and cheesy sauces very well because milk may scald or curdle quickly, and cheese can get watery and even congeal. When using dairy products to make a creamy or cheesy recipe, always add the dairy ingredients when the cooking cycle has complete already.

9. Be Prepared to Thicken:

The Instant Pot is capable of retaining liquid, so you should not expect your Instant Pot to lose much liquid or moistness. This may have a negative effect when you end up with dishes that have a much liquid. Add a bit of cornstarch mixed with water to help thicken up the dish. Always add the thickener towards the end of the cooking cycle because the cornstarch or thickening agent can actually interfere with the steam being built by the Instant Pot.

Instant Pot Must-Have Accessories

The Instant Pot comes along with lots of accessories. You might need to buy more accessories to get the most out of your meals:

1. **Silicone Egg Mold:**

The silicon egg mold will fit in your 5, 6, 8-quart pressure cookers. It can be used for storing smaller portions of dishes and includes a sealing lid.

2. **Silicone Mini Mitts:**

It is advisable to protect your fingers with the mini mitts. The cooking pot usually gets hot when cooking, the mini mitts set can be used to protect your hands when lifting items out of your pressure cooker.

3. **Silicone Vegetable Steamer and Lifter:**

The steamer / lifter keeps your veggies off the heated bottom of your pressure cooker. The steamer handles can be used to lift items easily from your pressure cooker. It also works great in your microwave. It can be used to lift a whole chicken out of your Instant Pot without the chicken falling apart.

4. **7-inch Spring Form Non-Stick Pan:**

The spring form pan can be used for baking. It can be used for baking cakes, cheesecakes, and bread. These sizes will fit into your pressure cooker 5, 6, 8 quarts.

5. **Cook's Stainless-Steel Steamer Basket / Colander:**

Most pressure cookers don't come with this basket! These tool helps to keep your food items off the bottom of the pressure cooker and out of the water. Food items such as pasta do not require draining when cooking in a pressure cooker but having the pasta in this basket helps to easily lift the pasta from the pressure cooker.

6. **Clear lid:**

The clear lid comes with a steam vent and handle. It is used for sautéing or slow-cooking. It comes in different sizes such as 3, 6, and 8-quart sizes.

7. **Extra Silicone Rings:**

The extra silicone rings are needed on hand at all times. It can be used to switch out rings depending on whether you're cooking a sweet or savory dish. They usually wear out after multiple uses, but it's advisable to have an extra at hand.

8. **Steaming Rack:**

The steaming rack can be used to steam your veggies, pot-stickers and proteins in your pressure cooker.

9. **Mesh steaming basket:**

This is another helpful variation of a steamer. The mesh steaming basket can be used for steaming, frying and straining in your pressure cooker. It can be used for multiple purposes.

10. **Extra Stainless Steel:**

It makes it easier to prepare multiple dishes. You just have to switch out the pots rather than cleaning one over and over again.

11. **Cheesecake pan:**

The cheesecake pan can be used for making cheesecake in your Instant Pot. The bottom is removable but doesn't leak and can be used for dessert after steaming all the veggies.

12. **Instant Read Digital Meat Thermometer:**

This thermometer can be used for measuring the heat content in your meat while pressure cooking. Having the Meat Thermometer on hand puts an end to serving undercooked or over cooked meat. The meat thermometer can also be used for daily cooking or grilling.

Cleaning Tips for Your Instant Pot

It is important to clean your Instant Pot right after dinner or right after you're done using it, because:

- The spills, drips, etc. are still warm and clean up more easily when cleaning right away.
- You'll appreciate your Instant Pot being clean the next time you're ready to use it.

What NOT to do when cleaning your Instant Pot:

Ensure that you clean your Instant Pot right after cook and avoid the following practices when cleaning:

- Do not submerge the base of your Instant Pot in water.
- Do not leave it plugged in while cleaning it.

Tools you will need when cleaning your Instant Pot include:

- Washcloth
- Non-scratch scouring pad
- Towel
- Dish soap or all-purpose spray cleaner
- Vinegar
- Baking soda
- Toothbrush or any other small cleaning brushes

How to Clean Your Instant Pot:

1. Fill your sink with hot and soapy water. This step is the most important because it will make the cleaning easier and faster.

2. Always ensure that you unplug your Instant Pot and remove the insert pot from the base of your Instant Pot.

3. Place every accessory that requires cleaning in the hot, soapy water. Dump out any liquid that must have accumulated in the condensation cup. Place the silicone ring, valve cover if your model has a removable valve cover, sealing valve, and lid in the soapy water.

4. Dip a small toothbrush or cleaning brush in the hot, soapy water. Use the small brush to clean all the nooks and crannies of the base. Make use of a wet, worn out cloth in sopping up any liquids or dislodged food particles in your Instant Pot. The toothbrush and washcloth can be used to reach and dislodge any stuck food particles.

5. Use a washcloth and all-purpose spray cleaner to wipe down the outside of your Instant Pot to look pretty and shiny.

6. Wash the accessories that's been soaking in the hot, soapy water. After washing, rinse and air dry with the towel.

7. Make use of the toothbrush to scrub the silicone ring. Use baking soda to remove any odor and staining. You can soak the silicon ring in vinegar water for a few hours. Rinse and air dry after washing.

8. Scrub the inside of the insert pot in circular motion with non-scratch scouring pad. Make use of baking soda for stubborn messes.

9. Scrub the following accessories with a small toothbrush — the lid, sealing valve, condensation cup and wipe with a towel to dry.

Frequently Asked Questions – FAQ
Before Purchasing Your Instant Pot

The answers to Frequently Asked Questions before purchasing an Instant Pot are listed below:

1. What is an Instant Pot? Is it the same as a pressure cooker?

Yes, the Instant Pot is the same as the pressure cooker and is currently one of the most popular electric pressure cooker models. It is a multi-functional cooker and has some extra functions such as rice cooker, soup, poultry, meat, yogurt, sauté pan etc.

2. Does the Instant Pot really speed up the cooking process?

Pressure cooking is always faster and saves time and energy. The fast cooking process of the pressure cooker may not be noticeable for some foods like broccoli or shrimps. Foods such as pulled pork can be cooked in less than 90 minutes, while it usually takes about 2 to 4 hours to make in the oven.

3. Are there any disadvantages with cooking in the Instant Pot?

The disadvantage of pressure cooking with pressure cookers is that you can't inspect, taste, or adjust the food along the way the cooking cycle. That's why it's necessary to follow the exact recipes instructions with accurate cooking times.

4. Is Instant Pot safe to use?

Most modern electric pressure cookers like the Instant Pot are quiet, very safe and easy to use. The Instant Pot has about 10 different safety mechanisms to avoid some of the potential issues. It has lots of safety features to prevent potential issues.

5. What is Instant Pot's working pressure?

The Instant Pot working pressure is within the range of 10.15~11.6 psi.

6. Can Instant Pot be used for Pressure Canning?

No, the Instant Pot has not been tested for food safety in pressure canning. The cooking features in Instant Pot IP-CSG, IP-LUX and IP-DUO series are regulated by a pressure sensor instead of a thermometer. Hence, the elevation of your location can disrupt the actual cooking temperature. For that very reason, it is not advisable to use your Instant Pot for pressure canning purpose.

7. Can I use the Instant Pot for Pressure Frying?

We would not recommend pressure frying in any electric pressure cookers. The pressure cooker gasket may be melted by the splattering of hot frying oil.

After Purchasing Your Instant Pot

What kind of Instant Pot accessories do you recommend?

There is hand-picked list of accessories we would recommend. The accessories include steamer baskets, meat thermometers, silicon egg mold, cheesecake pan, steaming rack etc.

2. What kind of accessories or containers can I use in the Instant Pot?

Any oven-safe accessories and containers can be used in your Instant Pot. Always have in mind that different materials will conduct heat differently and this will make the cooking times to vary. Always use stainless steel containers as because they easily conduct heat.

3. I just got my Instant Pot. What should I do first?

Congratulations and welcome to the party! Conduct an initial test run before cooking with your Instant Pot.

4. How to do a Quick Release?

When the cooking cycle is up, carefully move the venting knob from sealing position to venting position. It usually takes a few minutes and rapidly releases the pressure in the pressure cooker. Exercise some patient and wait until the floating valve completely drops before opening the lid.

5. How to do a Natural Release?

When the cooking cycle is up, you have to wait until the floating valve completely drops before opening the lid. Carefully turn the venting knob from sealing position to venting position. It will enable all the pressure to release before opening the lid. Natural pressure release usually takes about 10 – 25 minutes.

BREAKFAST
Banana Walnut Steel Cut Oats

Serves: 4

Preparation time: 5 minutes

Cook time: 20 minutes

Total time: 25 minutes

Ingredients:

- 1 cup steel cut oats
- 2 cups of water
- 1 cup of unsweetened almond milk
- ¼ cup of walnuts, chopped fine
- 2 tbsp. of ground flaxseeds (flaxseed meal)
- 2 tbsp. of chia seeds
- 1 large ripe banana, mashed
- 2 tbsp. of pure maple syrup
- 1 tsp. of ground cinnamon
- 1 tsp. of pure vanilla extract
- A dash of salt
- Topping ideas: Chopped toasted walnuts, Banana slices, A sprinkle of ground and nut milk

Cooking Instructions:

1. Add all ingredients into the bottom of your Instant Pot except the toppings.

2. Give everything a good stir to combine. Secure the lid on the pot.

3. Select Manual High Pressure to cook for about 10 minutes.

4. Quick release the pressure when the time is up. Flip the oats into bowls.

5. Serve immediately with optional toppings if desired.

Mexican Egg Casserole

Preparation time: 10 minutes

Cook time: 25 minutes

Total time: 35 minutes

Serves: 8

Ingredients:

- 8 large eggs, well-beaten
- 1 lb. of mild ground sausage
- ½ large red onion, chopped
- 1 red bell pepper, chopped
- 1 can of black beans, rinsed
- ½ cup of green onions
- ½ cup flour
- 1 cup of Cotija cheese
- 1 cup of mozzarella cheese
- Sour cream, cilantro to garnish (optional)

Cooking Instructions:

1. Turn on the Sauté feature and add the sausage and onion when hot.

2. Cook for about 6 minutes until the sausage is cooked through. Mix flour with eggs until everything is well combined.

3. Add the egg mixture to the sausage and onions into your Instant Pot. Add the chopped vegetables, beans and cheeses.

4. Set aside a little amount of mozzarella cheese. Secure the lid on top of the Instant Pot. Select Manual High Pressure for 20 minutes.

5. Use a natural pressure release when the timer beeps. Remove the casserole out of the Instant Pot. Carefully flip the casserole onto your serving plate.

6. Add the rest of the cheese on top of the casserole. Allow it to rest for some minutes until the cheese melted. Serve and enjoy!

Bacon Ranch Potatoes

Serves: 6

Preparation time: 10 minutes

Cook time: 7 minutes Total

time: 17 minutes

Ingredients:

- 2 pounds (1kg) red potatoes, scrubbed
- 3 bacon strips
- 2 tsp. of dried parsley
- 1 tsp. of kosher salt
- 1 tsp. of garlic powder
- 4 ounces (115gr) cheddar cheese, shredded
- 1/3 cup (80ml) Ranch dressing

Cooking Instructions:

1. Cut the potatoes into about 1-inch pieces and cut the bacon into small pieces.
2. Select the "Sauté" function and add bacon. Cook until nice and crisp.
3. Stir in potatoes, dried parsley, garlic powder and salt. Pour the 1/3 cup of water.
4. Secure the lid in place. Select Manual High Pressure for 7 minutes.
5. Do a quick pressure release and carefully remove the lid.
6. Add the ranch dressing and cheese. Give everything a good stir to combine.
7. Serve immediately and enjoy!

Vanilla Latte Steel Cut Oats

Servings: 4

Preparation time: 10 minutes

Cook time: 10 minutes

Total time: 20 minutes

Ingredients:

- 2 ½ cups of water
- 1 cup of milk
- 1 cup of steel cut oats
- 2 tbsp. of sugar
- 1 tsp. of espresso powder
- ¼ tsp. of salt
- 2 tsp. of vanilla extract
- Freshly whipped cream
- Finely grated chocolate

Cooking Instructions:

1. Add together the water, milk, oats, sugar, espresso powder, and salt into the bottom of your Instant Pot.

2. Give everything a good stir to dissolve espresso powder. Secure the lid in place. Select Manual High Pressure for 10 minutes.

3. Use a natural pressure release for 10 minutes, then quick release any remaining pressure.

4. Carefully open the lid and stir vanilla extract and additional sugar to taste.

5. Cover and allow to sit for about 5 minutes until the oats desired thickness is achieved.

6. Serve topped with whipped cream and grated chocolate.

French Toast Casserole

Preparation time: 10 minutes

Cook time: 15 minutes Total

time: 25 minutes

Ingredients:

- 3 eggs
- 1 cup of half and half cream
- ½ cup of milk
- 1 tbsp. of cinnamon
- 1 tsp. of vanilla
- 1 loaf of French bread cubed
- ½ cup of blueberries more to taste

Cooking Instructions:

1. Spray the insert of your Instant Pot with cooking spray.

2. Cube bread and add into the Instant Pot. Whisk together the milk, cream, cinnamon, vanilla and eggs.

3. Pour the custard mixture over the bread cubes and stir to coat.

4. Sprinkle in the blueberries. Secure the lid on top the Instant Pot.

5. Select Manual High Pressure for 15 minutes. Use a natural pressure release.

6. Carefully open the lid and serve immediately.

Buckwheat Porridge

Preparation time: 8 minutes

Cooking time: 30 minutes

Total time: 38 minutes

Servings: 6

Ingredients:

- 1 cup of raw buckwheat
- 3 cups of rice milk
- 1 sliced banana
- ¼ cup of raisins
- 1 tsp. ground cinnamon
- ½ tsp. vanilla

Cooking Instructions:

1. Rinse buckwheat well and put in Instant Pot.
2. Add all the ingredients.
3. Close and lock the lid in place and ensure that the valve is in sealing position.
4. Press the Manual key to cook on High Pressure for about 6 minutes.
5. When the time is up, use a natural pressure release for about 20 minutes.
6. Carefully open lid and stir porridge with a long-handled spoon.
7. Serve and enjoy.

Jamaican Cornmeal Porridge

Servings: 4

Preparation time: 5 minutes

Cook time: 20 minutes

Total time: 25 minutes

Calories: 241 kcal

Ingredients:

- 4 cups of water, separated
- 1 cup of milk
- 1 cup of yellow cornmeal, fine
- 2 sticks cinnamon
- 3 pimento berries
- 1 teaspoon of vanilla extract
- ½ teaspoon of nutmeg, ground
- ½ cup of sweetened condensed milk

Cooking Instructions:

1. Press the Porridge function to cook for about 6 minutes.

2. Pour 3 cups of water and 1 cup milk into the bottom of your Instant pot.

3. In another bowl, whisk 1 cup of water and cornmeal until fully combined. Pour the mixture to the Instant Pot and whisk.

4. Add the cinnamon sticks, pimento berries, vanilla extract, and nutmeg.

5. Secure the lid in place. Select Manual High Pressure for about 6 minutes.

6. Use a natural pressure release. Carefully open the lid and add sweetened condensed milk to sweeten.

7. Serve and enjoy!

Breakfast Burrito Casserole

Preparation time: 10 minutes

Cook time: 13 minutes

Total time: 23 minutes

Serves: 6 tacos

Ingredients:

- 4 eggs
- 2 lbs. of red potatoes, cubed
- ¼ cup of chopped white or yellow onion
- 1 diced jalapeno
- 6 ounces ham steak cubed
- ½ teaspoon of salt
- ½ teaspoon of mesquite seasoning
- ¼ teaspoon of chili powder
- ¾ teaspoon of taco seasoning
- Burrito toppings: Salsa, avocado, hot sauce and marinated red onions.

Cooking Instructions:

1. In a medium bowl, mix together the salt, seasonings and eggs and 1 tbsp. of water. Gently beat the eggs until the yokes are broken up.

2. Add the onions, potatoes or cheese, ham and jalapeno to the bowl. Add the mixture into the bottom of your Instant Pot.

3. Pour 1 cup of water to the bottom of your instant pot. Place the trivet and add the covered pan with the egg mixture on top the trivet.

4. Secure the lid in place. Select Manual High Pressure for 13 minutes. Use a natural pressure release.

5. Carefully open the lid and remove the pan from your Instant Pot. Fill the burritos. In a skillet, heat up the tortillas for some seconds on each side.

6. Add a few scoops of the egg mixture, a slice of avocado, salsa and red onions in each burrito.

7. Wrap up and enjoy.

Green Chile Breakfast Tacos

Ingredients:

- Instant Pot Green Chile
- 2 - 3 pounds of pork shoulder
- ¾ cup of chicken broth
- 1 14 ounces can roasted crushed tomatoes
- 2 mild hatch green chilies
- 2 hot hatch green chilies
- 1 onion, chopped
- 3 tablespoons of lard or bacon fat
- 1 ½ teaspoon of cumin
- Salt and pepper to taste

Breakfast Tacos:

- 8 ounces of green chilies
- 3 eggs, scrambled
- 2 Siete Foods Tortillas or any other paleo tortilla
- Sliced avocado, mayo, cilantro and lime wedges for garnish

Cooking Instructions:

1. Generously season the pork with salt, pepper and cumin and set aside.

2. Press the Sauté function on High and melt the lard. When the lard has melted, sauté the onions until browned.

3. Season the pork on all sides until nice crust. Remove pork from your Instant Pot. Deglaze the pot with chicken broth and scrape any brown bits with a wooden spoon.

4. Add the green chilies, diced tomatoes and pork. Secure the lid in place. Select Manual High Pressure for 90 minutes.

5. Use a natural pressure release. Carefully remove the lid and shred pork using two forks.

6. Serve and enjoy!

Vanilla Apple Cinnamon Breakfast Quinoa

Servings: 4

Preparation time: 5 minutes

Cook time: 1 minute

Total time: 6 minutes

Ingredients:

- 1 cup of quinoa
- 1 cup of water
- ¼ teaspoon of mineral salt
- 1 chopped apple
- 2 teaspoons of cinnamon
- ½ teaspoon of vanilla
- ¼ cup of gentle sweet

Cooking Instructions:

1. Add all ingredients into the bottom of your Instant Pot.

2. Give everything a good stir and secure the lid in place.

3. Select Manual High Pressure for 1 minute.

4. Do a natural pressure release for about 8 minutes when the timer beeps.

5. Carefully remove the lid and serve!

Spiced Pumpkin Apple Butter

Preparation time: 7 minutes

Cooking time: 13 minutes

Total time: 20 minutes

Yield: 5-6 Cups

Servings: 4

Ingredients:

- 1 tbsp. spice of pumpkin pie
- 2 cans pumpkin puree (17oz each)
- Fingertip of salt
- 5 apples, peeled and sliced into tiny pieces
- 1 bottle of hard apple cider (14oz)
- 1 cup of white sugar
- ¼ cup honey

Cooking Instructions:

1. In a medium bowl, whisk together all your ingredients until it blends.

2. Close and lock the lid in place and ensure that the valve is in sealing position.

3. Press the manual button to cook on high pressure for about 13 minutes.

4. When the time is up, use a natural pressure release for about 15 minutes.

5. Carefully open the lid once the pressure has been released.

6. Take out your butter and allow it cool completely then get some containers, put the butter according to your desired quantity and put them in your refrigerator.

7. Serve and enjoy!

Breakfast Quinoa

Preparation time: 20 minutes

Cooking time: 5 minutes

Total time: 25 minutes

Servings: 5

Ingredients:

- 2 cups of well rinsed uncooked quinoa
- ½ tsp. vanilla
- 3 cups of water
- fingertip of salt
- 2 tbsp. maple syrup
- 1/3 tsp. ground cinnamon

Optional Toppings: milk, fresh berries, sliced almonds

Cooking Instructions:

1. In a medium bowl, mix together the quinoa with water, maple syrup, vanilla, cinnamon, and salt. Add the mixture into the Instant Pot.

2. Close and lock the lid in place and ensure that the valve is in sealing position.

3. Press the Manual function to cook on High Pressure for about 5 minutes.

4. When the time is up, use a natural pressure release for about 10 minutes.

5. Carefully open the lid turning it away from you to allow steam to disperse.

6. Add the hot quinoa in a plate and top with milk, berries, and sliced almonds.

7. Serve and enjoy!

SOUPS & STEWS
Red Pepper Tomato Soup

Preparation time: 10 minutes

Cook time: 5 minutes

Total time: 15 minutes

Ingredients:

- 1 tbsp. of butter
- 1 tbsp. of oil
- 2 white onions, diced
- 2 red bell peppers, diced
- 3 cloves garlic
- 4 medium tomatoes, diced
- 2 tsp. of herbes de provence
- ½ tsp. of paprika
- ¼ tsp. of cayenne pepper
- 2-3 cups of bone or vegetable broth
- ½ tsp. of salt
- ½ tsp. of pepper
- Parsley or Cilantro for garnish

Cooking Instructions:

1. Press the Sauté function and add the butter and oil.

2. Sauté the onions for a couple of minutes until softened.

3. Mince the garlic gloves and add to the Instant Pot. Add the red peppers and diced tomatoes. Add the herbes de provence, paprika, cayenne pepper, salt, and pepper.

4. Give everything a good stir to combine and cook for about 3 minutes. Pour 2 cups of broth and stir. Secure the lid in place.

5. Select Manual High Pressure for 5 minutes. Do a quick pressure release and blend the soup with immersion blender.

6. Add rest of the broth to achieve your desired consistency. Season with additional salt and pepper to taste.

7. Serve with your desired toppings like cucumbers, onions, squash, zucchini, cheese and sour cream.

8. Serve immediately and enjoy!

Italian Sausage Stew

Preparation time: 10 minutes

Cook time: 3 minutes

Total time: 13 minutes

Ingredients:

- 2 tablespoons of butter
- ½ pound of pastured ground pork
- ½ teaspoon of onion powder
- ½ teaspoon of garlic powder
- 1½ teaspoon of basil
- ½ teaspoon of thyme ☐ ¼ teaspoon of cumin
- ½ teaspoon of marjoram
- ¼ teaspoon of cayenne
- 1 teaspoon of sea salt
- ¼ teaspoon of black pepper
- 1 medium onion, diced
- 2 carrots, diced
- 2 stalks of celery, diced
- 4 cloves of garlic, minced
- ½ cup white wine
- 1 – 15 ounces can organic diced tomatoes
- 2 quarts bone broth
- 2-3 large handfuls kale, chopped
- 8 ounces of gluten free noodles
- Sea salt/pepper to taste
- Freshly grated pram or other raw cheese to garnish

Cooking Instructions:

1. Set the Instant Pot to "Sauté" function. Add the butter once the pot is hot.

2. Add the pork and all of the seasonings. Give everything a good stir to combine and brown the meat.

3. Add the onion, carrot, celery, and garlic. Sauté the ingredients for about 6 minutes until the veggies are soft.

4. Deglaze the pan with the white wine scraping up any brown bits at the bottom.

5. Add the diced tomatoes, broth, kale and noodles and give everything a good stir to combine. Secure the lid in place.

6. Select Manual High Pressure for 3 minutes. Do a quick pressure release when the time is up.

7. Season with salt and pepper to taste and serve with freshly grated parmesan.

Chicken Tortilla Soup

Preparation time: 13 minutes

Cooking time: 5 minutes

Total time: 28 minutes

Servings: 7

Ingredients:

- 1 cup of black beans (salt less), drained and well rinsed
- 1 1/3 lb. raw chicken breasts (boneless skinless)
- 13 oz. chopped tomatoes with green chilies
- 15 oz. chopped tomatoes (salt less)
- 1 cup of frozen corn dissolved
- 1 jalapeno chopped
- 2 cloves garlic finely chopped
- 1 tsp. ground cumin
- 1/3 tsp. black pepper
- 1 tsp. chili powder
- 1 medium onion chopped
- 1 tsp. Himalayan salt
- 5 cups of organic chicken stock, low sodium

Tortilla Strips:

- Olive oil cooking spray
- 6 organic corn tortillas
- Himalayan salt

Optional toppings: Avocado, cheese, lime, Greek yogurt, cilantro

Cooking Instructions:

1. Put all the ingredients for the soup into your Instant Pot and stir to mix properly.

2. Close and lock the lid in place and ensure that the valve is in sealing position. Press the manual setting to cook on high pressure for about 20 minutes.

3. When the time is up, use a natural pressure release for about 15 minutes. Carefully open the lid and shred the chicken with two forks.

4. Serve and enjoy with optional toppings!

Spanish Infused Chicken Stew

Preparation time: 10 minutes

Cook time: 3 hours

Total time: 3 hours 10 minutes

Ingredients:

- 4 large chicken breasts, cut into chunks
- 4 cloves of garlic, minced
- ½ cooking chorizo, chopped roughly
- 2 carrots, chopped roughly
- 2 courgettes, chopped roughly
- 2 leeks, chopped roughly
- 3 red skinned potatoes, scrubbed and chopped in half
- 1 can of cannellini beans
- 1 handful of parsley, roughly chopped
- Small handful of oregano, finely chopped
- Glass of fino sherry or dry white wine
- A large pinch of smoked paprika
- A couple of strands of saffron
- Salt and pepper to taste
- Enough chicken stock to cover the chicken and vegetables

Cooking Instructions:

1. Prepare the vegetables and add them into your Instant Pot.

2. Heat a little oil in a sauté pan and cook the garlic, chicken and chorizo until the chicken is browned.

3. Add the chicken, chorizo and garlic mixture into the bottom of your Instant Pot and give everything a good stir.

4. Lightly heat the stock and add the herbs. Add the spices and seasonings and pour over the chicken to cover it. Secure the lid in place.

5. Select Slow Cook for 3 hours. Use a natural pressure release and carefully open the lid. Taste for seasoning and ladle the stew into serving bowls.

6. Serve with crusty bread or rice and enjoy!

Butternut Cauliflower Soup

Preparation time: 5 minutes

Cook time: 25 minutes

Total time: 30 minutes

Servings: 6 cups

Ingredients:

- 1 onion, diced
- 1-2 teaspoon of oil
- 2-3 cloves of garlic, minced
- 1 pound of frozen cauliflower
- 1 pound of frozen cubed butternut squash
- 2 cups of vegetable broth (chicken broth)
- 1 teaspoon of paprika
- ½ - 1 teaspoon of dried thyme
- ¼ - ½ teaspoon of red pepper flakes
- ¼ teaspoon of sea salt, plus extra to taste
- ½ cup of half and half, milk, or cream
- Toppings: Grated cheddar cheese, crumbled bacon, Sriracha or hot sauce, parmesan, sour cream, cheddar, and chives, chopped green onions, pumpkin seeds

Cooking Instructions:

1. Turn on the Sauté function on your Instant Pot and heat oil.

2. Sauté the onion until tender and golden. Add the garlic, cauliflower, butternut, veggie broth, and spices.

3. Secure the lid in place. Select Manual High Pressure for 5 minutes.

4. Use a quick pressure release for about 15 minutes when the timer beeps.

5. Carefully open the lid and add the half and half. Blend the soup with immersion blender or allow soup to cool and blend in batches with your blender or food processor.

6. Serve with your desired topping and enjoy!

Beef Lentil Stew

Preparation time: 10 minutes

Cook time: 20 minutes

Total time: 30 minutes

Ingredients:

- 1 lb. beef, cut into small cubes
- 1 cup of dry lentils
- 1 onion, diced
- 2-4 potatoes, peeled and diced
- 1 cup of carrots, diced
- 5 cloves of garlic, minced
- 4 cups of beef stock
- 1 (28 ounces) can diced tomatoes, with juice
- Salt and pepper, to taste
- 4 tablespoons of brown gravy mix

Cooking Instructions:

1. Cut the beef into small cubes.

2. Add the chopped onions, beef, carrots, garlic, and potatoes into the bottom of your Instant Pot.

3. Add the dry lentils, canned tomatoes, beef stock, and brown gravy mix.

4. Secure the lid in place. Select Manual High Pressure to cook for 20 minutes.

5. Do a natural pressure release and carefully remove the lid.

6. Serve and enjoy!

Stuffed Pepper Soup

Serves: 6

Preparation time: 5 minutes

Cook time: 25 minutes

Total time: 30 minutes

Ingredients:

- 1 tablespoon of extra virgin olive oil
- 3-4 cloves garlic, minced
- ½ onion, thinly sliced
- ½ can tomato paste ☐ 1 teaspoon of cumin
- 1 teaspoon of chili powder
- 1 teaspoon of black pepper
- 1 teaspoon of salt
- 2 bell peppers, sliced or diced
- ½ - 1 pound ground beef, uncooked
- 14.5 ounces can diced tomatoes
- 5 cups of beef broth
- 1 cup of organic brown rice, uncooked
- 3 tablespoons of cornmeal
- Parmesan cheese, for garnish
- Green onions, for garnish

Cooking Instructions:

1. Set the Instant Pot to Sauté function and add the ground beef. Add the garlic and onions until ground beef is cooked through and onions are soft.

2. Press OFF to cancel the Sauté function. Stir the tomato paste in with the ground beef, add the cumin, black pepper and salt. Add the peppers, diced tomatoes, and beef broth.

3. Give everything a good mix until combined. Add the rice and mix again. Secure the lid in place. Select Manual High Pressure for 23 minutes.

4. Use a natural pressure release and carefully open the lid. Add the cornmeal little by little and stir well. Ladle into bowls and garnish with parmesan cheese.

5. Serve with fresh dinner rolls or breadsticks and enjoy!

Andouille Sausage Stew

Preparation time: 10 minutes

Cook time: 10 minutes Total

time: 20 minutes

Ingredients:

- 1 lb. of uncooked Pork Andouille Sausage, crumbled
- 1 medium sweet onion, halved and thinly sliced
- ½ lb. of grape or cherry tomatoes
- 1 ½ lb. of Yukon Gold potatoes, peeled and cut into 1" pieces
- ¾ lb. of collard greens, stems removed and thinly sliced
- 1 cup of chicken broth
- 1 tsp. of kosher salt
- 20 - 25 turns freshly ground black pepper
- ½ medium lemon, freshly squeezed

Cooking Instructions:

1. Set Instant Pot to Sauté function and add the crumbled Andouille sausage.

2. Cook the sausage for about 5 to 8 minutes, stirring occasionally.

3. Add the sliced onions and tomatoes. Give everything a good mix and sauté for further 3 to 4 minutes.

4. Add the potatoes, collard greens and broth with salt and pepper to taste.

5. Secure the lid in place. Select Manual High Pressure for 10 minutes.

6. Use a natural pressure release and carefully open the lid. Finish by adding fresh lemon juice.

7. Serve and enjoy!

Cheeseburger Soup

Preparation time: 10 minutes

Cook time: 30 minutes Total

time: 40 minutes

Ingredients:

- 1 lb. lean ground beef
- 2 cups of chicken broth
- ½ cup of shredded carrots
- 2 cups of cubed potatoes
- 16 ounces can diced tomatoes
- 2 cups of heavy cream
- 16 ounces cheddar cheese
- 1 ounce American cheese
- ½ small onion, diced

Cooking Instructions:

1. Set the Instant Pot on Sauté.
2. Add the ground beef and sauté until brown and crumbled. Drain grease.
3. Add in chicken broth and veggies. Secure the lid in place.
4. Select Manual High pressure for 30 minutes. Use a quick pressure release.
5. Carefully open the lid and stir in heavy cream and cheese.
6. Serve and enjoy!

Beef & Butternut Squash Stew

Preparation time: 15 minutes

Cook time: 30 minutes

Total time: 45 minutes

Servings: 10

Ingredients:

- 1 large onion, chopped 2 cloves garlic, minced
- 2 celery stalks, chopped
- 2 carrots, chopped
- 2 tablespoons of tomato paste
- 1 tomato peeled and chopped
- 2 pounds of beef stew cut in 1" pieces
- 4 tablespoons of arrowroot starch
- 6 cups of peeled and chopped butternut squash cut in 1" cubes
- ½ cup of Marsala wine
- 2 ½ cup of beef broth
- 3 tablespoons of extra virgin olive oil
- 2 bay leaves
- 1 teaspoon of sweet Hungarian paprika
- 1 teaspoon of thyme
- 1 teaspoon of rosemary

Cooking Instructions:

1. Add 1 tablespoon of olive oil into the bottom of your Instant Pot.

2. Add the onions, garlic, celery, carrots, tomato and tomato paste. Generously season with salt and freshly ground black pepper.

3. Season the beef stew with salt, black pepper and 4 tablespoons of arrowroot starch (or cornstarch).

4. Add the beef and butternut squash. Season butternut squash with salt and freshly ground black pepper.

5. Season with sweet Hungarian paprika, thyme, rosemary and add 2 bay leaves. Pour the wine and beef broth, and the rest of the 2 tablespoons of olive oil.

6. Secure the lid in place. Select the Meat/Stew button and cook on High Pressure for 30 minutes.

7. Do a quick pressure release and carefully open the lid.

8. Serve and enjoy!

Hearty Broccoli Soup

Preparation time: 30 minutes

Cook time: 6 minutes

Total time: 36 minutes

Serves: 8-10

Ingredients:

- 1 tablespoon of vegan margarine or vegetable oil
- 1 small white onion, diced
- 3 cloves garlic, diced
- 64 ounces mushroom broth
- 1 cup of water
- 1 cup of unsweetened almond milk, or other unsweetened non-dairy milk
- 2 large bunches of broccoli (4 heads), florets only
- 1 head of cauliflower, florets only
- 1 medium sized Japanese Yam or Yukon gold potato, peeled and cut into chunks
- 2 cups of prepared brown rice
- 1 pkg. Beyond Meat Lightly Seasoned Chicken Strips, thawed and diced
- 1 chicken flavored bouillon cube
- 2 tablespoons of low sodium Tamari (or gluten free lite soy sauce)
- ½ teaspoon of salt
- 3 teaspoons of nutritional yeast
- 1 teaspoon of pike seasoning
- A pinch of black pepper

Cooking Instructions:

1. Add the margarine to your Instant Pot insert, and select the Sauté function.

2. Once the margarine melts, add the diced onion. Cook the ingredients until softened, stirring occasionally.

3. Add the garlic and sauté for additional 1 minutes. Press Cancel function and add the broccoli and cauliflower florets, and yam/potato.

4. Add the tamari, salt, pepper, Spike, nutritional yeast, and bouillon cube. Pour the broth, milk, and water into the bottom of your Instant Pot.

5. Secure the lid in place. Select Manual High Pressure for 6 minutes. Do a natural pressure release and carefully open the lid.

6. Puree the soup with your immersion blender. When your desired consistency is achieved, stir in your cooked brown rice and vegan chicken.

7. Allow it to sit for 10 minutes before serving.

Spicy Ethiopian Stew

Preparation time: 10 minutes

Cook time: 15 minutes Total

time: 25 minutes

Ingredients:

- 1½ cups of dried lentils
- 3 large garlic cloves, minced
- 3 tbsp. of tomato paste
- 3-5 tsp. of Berbere Spice
- 5 cups of vegetable broth
- 1 yellow onion, chopped
- 2 ½ cups of butternut squash, cut into chunks
- ½ tsp. of sea salt
- ½ tbsp. of maple syrup
- 2 tbsp. of pureed ginger
- 1/2 (10 oz.) bag chopped frozen spinach

Cooking Instructions:

1. Add all the ingredients into the bottom of your Instant Pot.

2. Secure the lid in place. Select Manual High Pressure for 15 minutes.

3. Do a natural pressure release for about 15 minutes.

4. Carefully open the lid and give everything a good stir.

5. Serve and enjoy!

POULTRY
Chicken Faux Pho

Preparation time: 15 minutes

Cook time: 30 minutes

Total time: 45 mins

Ingredients:

- 4 pounds of assorted chicken pieces bone-in and skin on
- 2 medium onions, quartered
- 1 inch ginger, peeled and roughly chopped
- 1 tbsp. of coriander seed
- 1 tsp. of green cardamom pods
- 1 black cardamom pod
- 1 cinnamon stick
- 4 cloves
- 1 lemon grass stalk trimmed and cut into 2 inch pieces
- ¼ cup of fish sauce
- 1 cup of fresh cilantro
- 1 head Bok choy, roughly chopped
- 1 large daikon root spiralized
- Sea salt to taste
- 2 jalapenos, thinly sliced
- ¼ onion, thinly sliced
- For Garnish: lime wedges, fresh basil and mung bean sprouts

Cooking Instructions:

1. In a dry skillet, add the coriander seeds. Toast over medium low heat for about 5 minutes until fragrant and golden brown.

2. Rinse the chicken pieces and add place them into your Instant Pot. Add the dry spices, cilantro, onion, lemon grass, and fish sauce.

3. Add enough cold water to cover the pot. Secure the lid in place. Select Manual High Pressure for 30 minutes.

4. Do a natural pressure release and carefully open the lid. Remove the chicken pieces and shred in a cutting board.

5. Strain the broth and add them back to your Instant Pot. Taste and adjust the seasoning with sea salt.

6. Bring to a simmer and add the Bok choy and spiralized daikon. Cook until tender for about 5 to 6 minutes.

7. Divide the noodles and shredded chicken into plates and ladle in the broth.

8. Serve with the garnishes and enjoy!

Mexican Chicken Soup

Preparation time: 10 minutes

Cook time: 20 minutes

Total time: 30 minutes

Ingredients:

- 3 boneless, skinless chicken breasts
- ¾ cup of sliced green onions
- 2 tsp. of chili powder
- 2 tsp. of ground cumin
- 1 tsp. of salt
- 1 tsp. of pepper
- 1 28 ounces can diced tomatoes
- 3 cups (24 ounces) chicken broth
- 1 15 ounces can black beans, drained and rinsed
- 1 10 ounces can diced tomatoes with green chilies
- 1 4 ounces can tomato paste
- 1 tbsp. of lime juice
- Toppings: sliced avocado, green onions, guacamole, sour cream, shredded cheese, tortilla chips

Cooking Instructions:

1. Add all the ingredients into the bottom of your Instant Pot except lime juice.

2. Secure the lid in place and ensure that the valve is in sealing position.

3. Select Manual function to cook for about 20 minutes if the chicken is still frozen and cook for about 12 minutes if the chicken was thawed.

4. Do a quick pressure release and carefully open the lid. Remove the chicken from Instant Pot and shred into bite size pieces.

5. Add the chicken back in your Instant Pot and stir in lime juice. Top with your preferred toppings.

6. Serve and enjoy!

Orange Chicken

Preparation time: 15 minutes

Cook time: 10 minutes

Total time: 25 minutes

Servings: 6 Calories:

383 kcal

Ingredients:

For the chicken:

- ¼ cup of cornstarch
- Salt and black pepper to taste (we added 1 tsp. salt + ½ tsp. of black pepper)
- 2 pounds of boneless skinless chicken breasts or thighs, cut into 1 1/2-inch pieces
- 4 tbsp. of vegetable oil
- 1 tbsp. of cornstarch + 1 tbsp. of water
- Sesame seeds to garnish (optional)
- Green onions, sliced (optional)

For the orange sauce:

- 1 cup of freshly squeezed orange juice (from 3-4 oranges)
- ¼ cup of granulated sugar
- 3 tbsp. of honey
- 1 tsp. of cornstarch
- 2 tbsp. of low-sodium soy sauce
- 1 tbsp. of rice vinegar
- 1 tbsp. of Chinese cooking wine Shaoxing wine
- 3 cloves garlic, minced
- 1 tsp. of sesame oil (we used toasted sesame oil)
- 1 tsp. of grated peeled fresh ginger
- ¼ tsp. of cayenne pepper
- 1 tbsp. of finely grated orange zest
- 1 tbsp. of cornstarch + 1 tbsp. of water

Cooking Instructions:

Make the sauce:

1. Zest 2 oranges and reserve the zest. In a medium bowl, add the orange juice, sugar, honey, soy sauce, vinegar, Chinese wine and garlic.

2. Add the sesame oil, ginger, cayenne pepper, and orange zest whisk together to combine. Set aside.

Make the chicken:

1. Add the cornstarch, salt, and pepper together in a gallon-sized zip-top bag. Add the chicken pieces, seal the bag, and shake to coat the chicken.

2. Press the "Sauté" function and add the oil when hot. Add the chicken in batches, and cook for about 2 minutes on each side or until the cornstarch slightly coated.

3. Transfer the chicken to a plate and repeat with any rest of the chicken. Select the Cancel function. Place the chicken to the pot and pour sauce over it.

4. Secure the lid in place and ensure that the valve is in sealing position. Select Manual High Pressure for 10 minutes.

5. Do a quick pressure release when the timer beeps. Carefully remove the lid. Turn the Sauté function and adjust heat to normal.

6. In a separate bowl, mix together the cornstarch and water until no lumps. Add the mixture over the chicken and mix to combine.

7. Simmer for about 2 minutes until the sauce thickens. Sprinkle with sesame seeds and sliced green onions, if desired.

8. Serve chicken with rice and enjoy!

Teriyaki Turkey Meatballs

Preparation time: 5 minutes

Cook time: 10 minutes

Total time: 15 minutes

Servings: 6

Calories: 244 kcal

Ingredients:

- 1 pound of ground turkey meat
- 5 saltine crackers, crushed
- 3 tbsp. of buttermilk
- ¼ cup of green onion, sliced + more for garnish
- 1 tsp. of garlic powder
- ½ tsp. of kosher salt
- Black pepper to taste
- 1 tbsp. of canola oil
- 1 tbsp. of sesame seeds

Teriyaki Sauce:

- ¾ cup of low sodium soy sauce
- 1/3 cup of rice vinegar
- 3 cloves garlic, minced
- 3 tsp. of fresh grated ginger
- 3 tbsp. of canola oil
- 4 ½ tbsp. of brown sugar
- ¼ tsp. of black pepper
- 1 tbsp. of corn starch

Cooking Instructions:

1. In a medium bowl, combine together the ground turkey, crushed crackers, buttermilk, green onions, garlic powder, salt, and pepper.

2. Gently shape into 16- 18 meatballs. In a separate bowl, combine together the teriyaki sauce ingredients and set aside.

3. Press the Sauté function on your Instant Pot and add the 1 tbsp. of oil. Sauté the meatballs for about 2 minutes on each side.

4. When brown add the teriyaki sauce. Secure the lid in place. Select Manual High Pressure for 10 minutes.

5. Do a natural pressure release for about 5 minutes. Sprinkle with sliced green onions and sesame seeds.

6. Serve with rice or quinoa and enjoy!

Chicken Paprika Stew

Preparation time: 10 minutes

Cook time: 25 minutes

Total time: 35 minutes

Serves: 4

Ingredients:

- 1 medium brown onion, diced
- 1 tbsp. of butter
- 1 tbsp. of olive oil
- 1 tsp. of salt
- 1.3 pound / 600 g diced chicken
- 3 tbsp. of paprika powder (mild or sweet)
- 2 large cloves of garlic, finely diced
- 1½ cups of chicken stock
- 1 tbsp. of tomato paste
- 2 heaped tbsp. of crème fraîche or sour cream
- ½ cup of frozen garden peas (thawed out in warm water)
- 1 tsp. of arrowroot flour/starch (or corn starch)
- More sour cream, to serve with if you desire
- Cucumber dill salad
- 2 medium cucumbers, sliced thinly
- 2 tbsp. of finely chopped dill
- 2 tbsp. of crème fraîche or sour cream
- Generous pinch of salt

Cooking Instructions:

1. Press the Sauté function and add the oil when hot.

2. Add the onion, butter, and salt and sauté for 5 minutes and stir occasionally.

3. Add the diced chicken and cook for additional two minutes. Add the paprika and garlic and stir again.

4. Add the chicken stock, tomato paste and crème fraîche or sour cream. Stir through. Press the Cancel function.

5. Secure the lid in place and ensure that the valve is in sealing position. Select Manual High Pressure for 12 minutes.

6. Do a natural pressure release, then quick release the remaining pressure. Carefully remove the lid and add the peas.

7. Sauté for about 5 minutes with the lid off, stirring occasionally. After 5 minutes, scoop ¼ cup of the sauce liquid into a small bowl.

8. Add the arrowroot flour (corn flour). Give everything a good whisk to dissolve. Turn off your Instant Pot and stir in the arrowroot liquid.

9. Add additional tablespoon of crème fraîche/sour cream to further thicken the sauce.

10. In a medium bowl, prepare the salad by combining all ingredients and serve alongside chicken paprika.

11. Serve and enjoy!

Honey Lemon Chicken

Preparation time: 12 minutes

Cooking time: 35 minutes

Total time: 47 minutes

Calories: 370 kcal

Servings: 4

Ingredients:

- 3 cloves garlic, peeled and diced
- 1 lb. bone-in, skin-on chicken thighs
- 1 1/2 tsp lemon pepper seasoning
- zest of one lemon
- 3 tbsp. honey
- 2 1/2 tbsp. water
- 1 tbsp. soy sauce
- 1 tsp. corn starch
- 1/3 cup of freshly squeezed lemon juice (about 1 lemon)
- 1/3 cup of water
- 2 tbsp. canola oil
- Corn starch Slurry for thickening of the sauce

Cooking Instructions:

1. Trim the chicken thighs of excess fat and season with lemon pepper seasoning.

2. Set the Instant Pot on sauté mode. Put oil when the pot is hot and heat with the Instant Pot lid open.

3. Keep chicken in a single layer with skin side down. Cook for about 3 minutes and then turn the other side of the chicken to cook for another 3 minutes.

4. Remove surplus oil from the Instant Pot, put garlic and cook. Stir for about 20 to 30 seconds.

5. Using a small bowl, mix lemon juice, lemon zest, honey, water, and soy sauce. Stir properly until well mixed and pour over chicken.

6. Close and lock the lid in place and ensure that the valve is in sealing position. Press the manual button to cook on high pressure for about 15 minutes.

7. When the time is up, use a natural pressure release for about 7 minutes. Carefully open the lid once the pressure has been released.

8. Serve and enjoy.

Ground Turkey Lentil Chili

Preparation time: 25 minutes

Cooking time: 20 minutes

Total time: 45 minutes

Servings: 5

Ingredients:

- 1 (10 oz.) can tomato sauce
- 2 lb. ground turkey
- 2 diced garlic cloves
- 2 tbsp. tomato paste
- ½ tsp. pepper
- 1 ½ tsp. salt
- 1 ½ cup of dry green lentils
- 2 cups of water
- 1 (12 oz.) can petite diced tomatoes
- 1 (4 oz.) can diced green chili
- 2 tsp. chili powder
- 1 tsp. cumin
- 1 medium yellow onion, diced

Cooking Instructions:

1. Switch your Instant Pot on to sauté. Fry the ground turkey to brown.

2. Put the minced onions, garlic, tomato paste and salt and cook until meat is browned and onions are soften.

3. Put the lentils, water, tomato sauce, diced tomatoes, green chili, chili powder, cumin and pepper. Close and lock the lid in place and ensure that the valve is in sealing position.

4. Press the manual key to cook on high pressure for about 15 minutes. When the time is up, use a natural pressure release for about 15 minutes.

5. Carefully remove the lid and scoop the chili into plates. Top with a dollop of sour cream and some diced green onions.

6. Serve and enjoy!

BEEF & PORK
Beef Masala Curry

Preparation time: 10 minutes

Cook time: 30 minutes

Total time: 40 minutes

Serves: 4

Ingredients:

- 2 pounds stewing beef, cut in 2 inch cubes
- 1 onion, chopped
- 3 garlic cloves, minced
- ½ cup of crushed tomatoes
- ¼ cup of fresh cilantro, chopped
- 1 teaspoon of salt
- 1 teaspoon of freshly ground black pepper
- 1 teaspoon of turmeric
- 1 tablespoon of garam masala
- ½ teaspoon of cumin
- ½ teaspoon of coriander
- ½ teaspoon of cayenne pepper
- ½ teaspoon of smoked paprika
- ½ teaspoon of lemon zest
- 1 teaspoon of brown sugar
- 1 tablespoon of oil
- 1 cup of beef stock

Cooking Instructions:

1. Press the Sauté function on your Instant Pot. When hot, add the oil, chopped onions, garlic, spices, salt and pepper.

2. Sauté the ingredients until the onions turns translucent, for about 3 minutes. Stir in the crushed tomatoes, brown sugar and bring to a boil.

3. Add the mixture into the food processor and blend to form paste. Brown the meat on each side, pour in the blended spice paste, stock and add lemon zest.

4. Secure the lid in place and ensure that the valve is in sealing position. Select Manual High Pressure for 30 minutes.

5. Serve with steamed rice and cilantro.

Pork Vindaloo

Servings: 6

Preparation time: 10 minutes

Cook time: 25 minutes Total

time: 35 minutes

Ingredients:

- 3 lb. (1.44 kg) boneless pork shoulder, cubed
- 1 tsp. of sea salt
- ¼ cup (60 ml) olive oil
- 1 large white onion, peeled and finely chopped
- 4 cloves garlic, peeled and minced
- 1 piece fresh ginger, peeled and grated
- 2 tbsp. of vindaloo seasoning or Madras curry
- 1 tsp. of hot paprika
- ½ tsp. of ground turmeric
- 3 tbsp. of all-purpose flour
- 1/3 cup (80 ml) Champagne vinegar
- 1 (14 ½ oz.) can diced tomatoes in juice, undrained
- 1 cup (250 ml) reduced-sodium chicken broth

Cooking Instructions:

1. Sprinkle cubed pork with a slat. Heat the 2 tbsp. of olive oil over medium-high heat.

2. Brown the meat in a single layer on all sides or about 6 minutes working in batches. Transfer the browned pork to a plate using a slotted spoon.

3. Add the chopped white onion and sauté, stirring occasionally until soft for about 3 minutes). Stir in garlic, ginger, and spices.

4. Cook, stirring for additional 30 seconds. Sprinkle in all-purpose flour and stir again. Place the browned pork to your Instant Pot.

5. Stir in vinegar, tomatoes with their juice and chicken broth. Scrape up any browned bits from the bottom of the pot. Bring the pot to a boil over medium-high heat.

6. Secure the lid in place and ensure that the valve is in sealing position. Select Manual High Pressure for 25 minutes.

7. Do a natural pressure release for about 15 minutes and carefully remove the lid. Skim any fat from the top of sauce and sprinkle with fresh chopped cilantro.

8. Serve immediately and enjoy!

Spicy Beef Stew

Preparation time: 5 minutes

Cook time: 40 minutes

Total time: 45 minutes

Ingredients:

- 2 tablespoons of ghee or avocado oil
- 1 pound of beef stew meat, cut into cubes
- 1 onion, diced
- 3 medium potatoes, chopped
- 4 carrots, chopped
- 2 celery stalks, chopped
- 2 cups of kale leaves, stems removed
- 1 teaspoon of garlic powder
- ½ teaspoon of black pepper
- 2 cups of bone broth
- 2 tablespoons of your favorite hot sauce
- Sea salt, to taste

Cooking Instructions:

1. Press the Sauté function on your Instant Pot and add avocado oil.

2. Add the meat and stir until the meat is browned. Add the remaining ingredients except salt and give everything a good stir.

3. Secure the lid in place. Select the Meat/Stew function for 40 minutes. Press the Cancel function to release the pressure when the timer beeps.

4. Carefully remove the lid and give everything a good stir. Taste and adjust the seasoning to taste with more salt.

5. Serve and enjoy!

Cuban Pulled Pork

Preparation time: 15 minutes

Cook time: 1 hour

Total time: 1 hour 15 minutes

Servings: 16

Calories: 111 kcal

Ingredients:

- 3 - 4 pound of pork shoulder
- 2 tsp. of salt, or more to taste
- 1 tsp. of black pepper, or more to taste
- 8 cloves garlic, crushed
- 2 leaves bay
- 1 tsp. of dried oregano
- 1 tsp. of ground cumin
- ½ cup of fresh orange juice (2 medium oranges approx.)
- ¼ cup of fresh lime juice (2 limes approx.)
- ¾ cup of vegetable stock
- Fresh chopped cilantro to garnish (optional)

Cooking Instructions:

1. Generously season the pork shoulder with salt and black pepper, rubbing in both sides.

2. Add the pork into the bottom of your Instant Pot. Add the garlic, bay leaves, oregano, cumin, orange juice, lime juice and vegetable stock.

3. Give everything a good mix to combine. Secure the lid in place and ensure that the valve is in sealing position.

4. Press the "Meat" function and adjust to cook for 60 minutes. Do a natural pressure release for about 10 minutes.

5. Carefully remove the lid and shred the pork with two forks, removing any excess fat, if necessary. Strain the cooking liquid from the pot.

6. Preheat oven broil and place it with a slotted spoon to a large baking sheet. Add a little bit of the leftover cooking juices evenly on top of the pork.

7. Broil the pork for about 4 minutes, or until the edges of the pork are brown and crispy. Sprinkle with chopped fresh cilantro.

8. Serve immediately and enjoy!

Beef Luau Stew

Preparation time: 10 minutes

Cook time: 25 minutes Total

time: 35 minutes

Ingredients:

- Luau leaves (taro leaves) stems & fibrous veins removed
- 8 cups of water
- A pinch of Hawaiian salt
- 3 pounds of chuck roast
- ½ onion, chopped
- 2 tablespoons of minced garlic
- 4 cups of chicken broth
- 2 cans of coconut milk
- Salt & pepper to taste

Cooking Instructions:

1. Wash and cut off stems of luau leaves. Chop the leaves and add into your Instant Pot along with 8 cups water.

2. Sprinkle with a pinch of Hawaiian salt and place the leaves into water. Secure the lid in place.

3. Select Manual High Pressure for 15 minutes. Do a natural pressure release for about 10 minutes.

4. Carefully remove the lid and discard the leaves. Cut the chuck roast into big chunks. Sauté meat with coconut oil. Add the sliced onions, garlic, 4 cups chicken broth, and cooked luau leaves.

5. Give everything a good stir to incorporate. Press the Cancel function sauté and select Meat/Stew function for 25 minutes.

6. Do a natural pressure release for about 10 minutes, then quick release any remaining pressure.

7. Carefully remove the lid and add the 2 cans of coconut milk and stir. Season to taste. Serve and enjoy!

Mexican Pulled Pork

Preparation time: 2 minutes

Cook time: 30 minutes

Total time: 32 minutes

Servings: 6

Calories: 331 kcal

Ingredients:

- 3-4 pounds of boneless pork roast, excess fat trimmed, cut into 2-inch chunks
- 1/3 cup of taco seasoning
- 1 cup of orange juice
- ½ cup of chicken stock
- ¼ cup of lime juice

Cooking Instructions:

1. Generously season the pork chunks on both sides with taco seasoning.

2. Add seasoned pork, orange juice, chicken stock and lime juice into the bottom of your Instant Pot.

3. Give everything a good mix to combine. Secure the lid in place. Select "Meat" function and adjust until time reads 30 minutes.

4. Do a natural pressure release for about 10 minutes. Carefully remove the lid and shred the pork with two forks. Preheat oven broil.

5. Transfer the pork with a slotted spoon to a large baking sheet. Spoon 1/3 - 1/2 of the leftover cooking juices evenly on top of the pork.

6. Broil the pork for about 4 minutes or until the edges of the pork are brown and crispy. Sprinkle with chopped fresh cilantro.

7. Serve immediately and enjoy!

Beef Stroganoff

Preparation time: 8 minutes

Cooking time: 25 minutes

Total time: 33 minutes

Calories: 321 kcal

Servings: 5

Ingredients:

- 1 tbsp. oil
- ½ cup of diced onions
- 1 tsp. pepper
- 1 tbsp. Worcestershire sauce
- 1 tsp. salt
- 1 lb. pork tips or beef stew meat
- ¾ cup of water
- 1 tbsp. garlic
- 1.5 cups of chopped mushrooms

For Finishing:

- ¼ cup sour cream
- 1/3 tsp xanthan gum (sub with arrowroot starch, corn starch or other thickener)

Cooking Instructions:

1. Switch Instant Pot on Sauté on high and add the oil.

2. Add onions and garlic when the oil is hot and stir for a while. Add all ingredients except sour cream and close up the pot.

3. Close and lock the lid in place and ensure that the valve is in sealing position. Select Manual function to cook on High Pressure for about 8 minutes.

4. When the time is up, use a natural pressure release for about 10 minutes. Carefully remove the lid and add the sour cream and stir.

5. Pour the xanthan gum a little at a time, and keep stirring until the mix thickens. Scoop into plates and top some cauliflower rice or low carb noodles. Serve.

Pork Carnitas

Preparation time: 10 minutes

Cook time: 1 hour 10 minutes

Total time: 1 hour 20 minutes

Servings: 6

Calories: 348 kcal

Ingredients:

- 2 ½ - 3 pounds of skinless, boneless pork shoulder
- 2 tbsp. of olive oil
- 2 tsp. of kosher salt
- ½ tsp. of black pepper
- 2 tsp. of oregano
- 2 tsp. of garlic powder ☐ 1 tsp. of onion powder
- 1 tsp. of cumin
- 1 tsp. of ground cinnamon
- 8 garlic cloves, minced
- ½ cup of orange juice (about 2 oranges)
- ¼ cup of lime juice (about 2 limes)
- 1 cup of chicken broth
- 2 bay leaves
- 1 onion, quartered
- Fresh cilantro, chopped to garnish

Cooking Instructions:

1. Rinse and pat dry pork with a paper towel. Trim excess fat and cut into 2-3 inches chunks.

2. Add the oil, salt, pepper, oregano, garlic powder, onion powder, cumin, cinnamon and minced garlic into the bottom of your Instant Pot.

3. Add the pork and toss everything to coat. Add the orange juice, lime juice, chicken broth, and bay leaves and give everything a good mix to combine.

4. Secure the lid in place. Select Meat/Stew function and adjust to read for about 45 minutes.

5. Do a natural pressure release for about 15 minutes. Carefully remove the lid and discard the bay leaves.

6. Serve and enjoy!

Beef and Broccoli

Preparation time: 10 minutes

Cook time: 20 minutes

Total time: 30 minutes

Servings: 8

Calories: 273 kcal

Ingredients:

Sauce:

- 2/3 cup of water
- 2 tbsp. of cornstarch
- ½ cup of low sodium soy sauce
- ¼ cup of brown sugar
- 2 tbsp. of Chinese cooking wine Shaoxing wine
- 1 tsp. of sesame oil
- 2 tbsp. of hoisin sauce (optional)
- 1 tablespoon oyster sauce
- 1 tsp. of ground white pepper or red pepper (cayenne)

Stir-fry:

- 2 pounds of round strips
- 3 tbsp. of vegetable oil, separated
- 4 cups of broccoli florets
- 3 garlic cloves, minced
- 1 tsp. of fresh ginger, minced
- ¼ cup of green onion, sliced (optional)
- 1 tsp. of sesame seeds to garnish (optional)

Cooking Instructions:

1. In a medium bowl, mix together all the sauce ingredients. Add the meat in a big bowl and add ¼ cup of sauce.

2. Give everything a good mix to combine. Allow it to marinade for about 20 to 25 minutes. Press the Sauté function, adjust heat to less. Once hot, add 1 tbsp. of oil.

3. Add the broccoli florets and cook for about 3 - 5 minutes, stirring constantly, until they are tender. Remove from Instant Pot and set aside. Press Cancel function.

4. Press the "Sauté" function, adjust heat to more. Add 2 tbsp. of oil. Once hot, add the garlic and ginger and cook for about 2 minutes, stirring constantly.

5. Add the meat working in batches and brown. When the meat is brown, add the rest of the sauce and give everything a good mix to combine.

6. Secure the lid in place. Select the "Meat" function, adjust the time to 15 minutes. Do a natural pressure release for about 5 minutes, then quick release any remaining pressure.

7. Carefully remove the lid and add broccoli to pot and toss to coat. Season with salt to taste. Garnish with green onion slices and sesame seeds.

8. Serve over rice or steamed vegetables and enjoy!

Hawaiian Pineapple Pork

Preparation time: 5 minutes

Cook time: 20 minutes

Total time: 25 minutes

Servings: 8

Calories: 384 kcal

Ingredients:

- 1 can (20 ounces) Pineapple chunks in pineapple juice
- 2 tbsp. of water
- 1 tbsp. of cornstarch
- 3 tbsp. of honey
- 2 tbsp. of soy sauce
- 2 tbsp. of brown sugar
- 1 tbsp. of grated ginger
- 3 garlic cloves, minced
- 2 tbsp. of olive oil, separated
- 1 onion, chopped
- 1 red pepper, chopped
- 2 pounds of boneless pork stew meat
- Kosher salt and black pepper
- 1 tsp. of oregano
- Parsley for garnishing

Cooking Instructions:

1. Drain the pineapple chunks and set the juice aside.

2. In a medium bowl, mix together the water, cornstarch, reserved pineapple juice, honey, soy sauce, brown sugar, ginger and garlic until well combined.

3. Turn the Instant Pot ON and press the "Sauté" function and adjust heat to more. Once hot, add the 1 tbsp. of oil.

4. Add the onion, red peppers and cook for about 3 minutes, stirring constantly, until they are tender. Remove the pork from your Instant Pot and set aside.

5. Add the rest of the tablespoon of oil to your Instant Pot. Once hot, add the pork meat and cook until no longer pink.

6. Add the pineapple chunks and oregano. Generously season with salt and black pepper to taste. Add the sauce and give everything a good stir to combine.

7. Secure the lid in place. Select Manual High Pressure for 10 minutes. Do a natural pressure release for about 15 minutes. Carefully remove the lid and add the reserved onions.

8. Add the red peppers and toss to coat. Taste and adjust seasoning with more salt and black pepper, if desired. Garnish with fresh chopped parsley, if desired.

9. Serve over rice or steamed vegetables and enjoy!

Boneless Pork Chops

Preparation time: 6 minutes

Cooking time: 9 minutes

Total time: 15 minutes

Servings: 5

Ingredients:

- 1 stick of margarine
- boneless pork chops
- 1 package of ranch mix
- 1 １/2 cup of water
- 1 tbsp. of coconut oil

Cooking Instructions:

1. Put the pork chops in the Instant Pot and add a tablespoons of coconut oil.
2. Switch on the sauté mode and fry to brown on both sides.
3. Add the margarine on top and stir in the ranch mix packet on top.
4. Pour water over the pork and put the lid on and set to sealing.
5. Close and lock the lid in place and ensure that the valve is in sealing position.
6. Press the Manual button to cook on High Pressure for about 7 minutes.
7. When the time is up, use a natural pressure release for about 5 minutes.
8. Carefully open the lid once the pressure has been released.
9. Serve immediately and enjoy.

Beef Pot Roast

Preparation time: 15 minutes

Cooking time: 1 hour 45 minutes

Total time: 2 hours

Servings: 7

Ingredients:

- 2 1/2 tbsp. corn starch
- 1 big bag carrots, peeled and chopped
- 4 1/2 (1 oz.) packets of McCormick Brown Gravy Mix
- 1 cup brewed coffee
- 10 oz. red wine (cabernet)
- ½ cup of reduced sodium soy sauce
- 3 tbsp. Worcestershire sauce
- 2 tsp. freshly cracked black pepper
- 3 lb. bottom round roast
- 6 big cloves garlic, diced
- 1 big sweet yellow onion, chopped
- 2 cups of sliced Portobello mushrooms
- 2 tbsp. oil

Cooking Instructions:

1. Whisk together McCormick Brown Gravy Mix and cornstarch in a big container. To avoid lumps, whisk in coffee gently.

2. Whisk in wine, soy sauce, Worcestershire sauce, garlic and black pepper. Keep them in one corner. Set Instant Pot to sauté mode.

3. Add the oil to pot and quickly sear meat on all sides. Switch off sauté mode.

4. Top meat with carrots, onion and mushrooms, gravy mix on top and keep lid on Instant pot with steam valve closed.

5. Close and lock the lid in place and ensure that the valve is in sealing position. Press the manual settings to cook on high pressure for about 45 minutes.

6. When the time is up, use a natural pressure release for about 15 minutes. Carefully remove roast from Instant Pot.

7. Shred the beef with two forks, put gravy and vegetables to mix well. Scoop your dish into a plate, top with gravy and vegetables over mashed potatoes.

8. Serve and enjoy!

FISH & SEAFOODS
Creamy Fish Chowder

Servings: 4

Preparation time: 5 minutes

Cook time: 5 minutes Total

time: 10 minutes

Ingredients:

- ¾ cup of chopped bacon
- 1 medium onion, chopped
- 2 ribs celery, chopped
- 1 medium carrot, chopped
- 2 cloves garlic, minced
- 3 cups Peeled & Cubed Potatoes, preferably Yukon gold
- 4 cups of chicken bone-broth or vegetable broth
- 2 tbsp. of butter (pasture raised, grass fed) or ghee
- 1 lb. wild caught Haddock Filets, FROZEN
- 1 cup of frozen or freeze dried corn
- Sea salt (real salt)
- Ground White Pepper
- 2 cups organic heavy cream
- 1 heaping tbsp. of organic potato starch

Cooking Instructions:

1. Select the Sauté function and cook bacon in butter until crispy.

2. Add the onion, garlic, carrot and celery. Sauté for about 3 minutes or until veggies are soft. Season with sea salt and white pepper.

3. Add the potatoes, corn, fish and broth. Secure the lid in place. Select Manual High Pressure for 5 minutes.

4. Do a natural pressure release and carefully remove the lid. Mix together the heavy cream and potato starch to combine. Add to chowder.

5. Give everything a good stir and cook for about 3 minutes to slightly thicken. Serve and enjoy!

Shrimp Paella

Preparation time: 10 minutes

Cook time: 5 minutes

Total time: 15 minutes

Servings: 4 Calories:

318 kcal

Ingredients:

- 1 pound of jumbo shrimp, shell and tail on frozen
- 1 cup of Jasmine rice
- 4 tablespoons of butter
- 1 onion, chopped
- 4 cloves garlic, chopped
- 1cred pepper, chopped
- 1 cup of chicken broth
- ½ cup of white wine
- 1 teaspoon of paprika
- 1 teaspoon of turmeric
- ½ teaspoon of salt
- ¼ teaspoon of black pepper
- 1 pinch saffron threads
- ¼ teaspoon of red pepper flakes
- ¼ cup of cilantro (optional)

Cooking Instructions:

1. Press the Sauté function on your Instant Pot. When hot, add the butter to melt.

2. Add the onions and sauté until softened. Add the garlic and sauté for additional 1 minute. Add the paprika, turmeric, salt, black pepper and red pepper flakes.

3. Add the saffron threads and cook for additional 1 minute, stirring. Add red peppers, rice and give everything a good stir.

4. Cook for about 1 minute and add the chicken broth and white wine. Ensure that all the rice is covered.

5. Place the shrimp on top. Secure the lid in place and ensure that the valve is in sealing position. Select Manual High Pressure for 5 minutes.

6. Do a quick pressure release and carefully remove the lid. Remove shrimp from pot and peel if desired.

7. Serve with Cilantro and enjoy!

Fish Tacos

Preparation time: 6 minutes

Cooking time: 7 minutes

Total time: 13 minutes

Servings: 5

Ingredients:

- 2 sprigs of fresh cilantro.
- 2 tilapia fillets
- Salt to taste
- 2 tbsp. of smoked paprika
- juice of one lime
- 1 tsp. of canola oil

Cooking Instruction

1. Use a large parchment paper and put tilapia in the middle.

2. Using canola oil paint the tilapia, spray with salt and paprika, squeeze lime juice on the tilapia and sprinkle with some cilantro.

3. Bend or fold your old parchment paper into a packet and keep no space for air ventilation.

4. Add 1 1/2 cups of water in the bottom of your Instant Pot, along with the trivet.

5. Close and lock the lid in place and ensure that the valve is in sealing position.

6. Press the Manual function to cook on High Pressure for about 7 minutes.

7. When the time is up, use a natural pressure release for about 5 minutes.

8. Cut the fish according to how you want to place it on a taco. Build your taco to your choice. Serve and enjoy!

Savory Shrimp with Tomatoes & Feta

Preparation time: 8 minutes

Cooking time: 15 minutes

Total time: 23 minutes

Calories: 280 kcal

Servings: 6

Ingredients:

Cook Together:

- 1 tsp. oregano
- 1 tbsp. garlic
- 1.5 cups of chopped onion
- 1 15 oz. can tomatoes
- 1 tsp. salt
- ½ tsp. red pepper flakes adjust to taste
- 1 lb. frozen shrimp 21-25 count, shelled
- 2 tbsp. Butter

Add after cooking:

- ¼ cup of sliced black olives
- 1 cup of crumbled feta cheese
- 1/3 cup of parsley

Cooking Instructions:

1. Set your Instant Pot to Sauté and put the butter when it is hot.

2. Allow it to melt a little and then put garlic and red pepper flakes, onions, tomatoes, oregano and salt and pour the frozen shrimp.

3. Close and lock the lid in place and ensure that the valve is in sealing position. Press the manual function to cook on low pressure for about 2 minutes.

4. When the time is up, use a natural pressure release for about 5 minutes. Mix in the shrimp with all the tomato broth. Allow it to cool for a while. Pour the feta cheese, olives, and parsley on top.

5. Serve and enjoy!

Shrimp and Lentil Stew

Preparation time: 10 minutes

Cook time: 12 minutes

Total time: 22 minutes

Servings: 6

Ingredients:

- 1 tbsp. of olive oil
- 3 cloves garlic, minced
- 1 onion, chopped small
- 1 red bell pepper, chopped
- 1 tbsp. of thyme
- 2 tsp. of oregano
- 2 tsp. of Old Bay Seasoning
- ½ tsp. of cayenne
- 1 cup of lentils
- 1 pound shrimp, deveined and peeled
- 3 cups of chicken broth (or vegetable)
- 1 15 ounces can diced tomatoes, drain slightly
- ½ cup of tomato sauce
- 2 tbsp. of Worcestershire sauce
- 1 cup of frozen riced broccoli

Cooking Instructions:

1. Turn on the "Sauté" function on your Instant Pot and add the olive oil.

2. Add the garlic, onion, and bell pepper and cook for about 5 minutes, or until ingredients are softened.

3. Add the thyme, oregano, Old Bay, and cayenne and toss everything to combine. Sauté for another 1 minute.

4. Add the lentils, shrimp, and chicken broth into your pot.

5. Add the diced tomatoes, tomato sauce, Worcestershire sauce and riced broccoli. Secure the lid in place. Select Manual High Pressure for 12 minutes.

6. Do a natural pressure release and carefully remove the lid. Taste and adjust the seasoning with salt and pepper. Serve and enjoy!

Shrimp Coconut Milk

Preparation time: 10 minutes

Cook time: 10 minutes

Total time: 20 minutes

Servings: 4 Calories:

192 kcal

Ingredients:

- 1 lb. shrimp shelled, deveined
- 1 tbsp. of minced ginger, minced
- 1 tbsp. of garlic, minced
- ½ tsp. of turmeric
- 1 tsp. of salt
- ½ tsp. of cayenne pepper
- 1 tsp. of garam masala
- ½ can of unsweetened coconut milk

Cooking Instructions:

1. In a medium bowl, mix together all the ingredients.

2. Add 2 cups of water into the inner liner of your Instant Pot and place the trivet.

3. Add the shrimp and coconut mixture in a pot that will fit inside your Instant Pot.

4. Cover the pot with a piece of foil. Secure the lid in place and ensure that the valve is in sealing position.

5. Set to cook on Low Pressure for about 4 minutes. Do a quick pressure release when the timer beeps.

6. Carefully open the lid and give everything a good mix. Add a little extra coconut milk if you desired.

7. Serve immediately and enjoy!

Coconut Red Curry Shrimp

Preparation time: 5 minutes

Cook time: 25 minutes

Total time: 30 minutes

Servings: 6

Ingredients:

For the Marinade:

- ¼ cup of coconut milk canned
- 1 teaspoon of cumin
- 1 teaspoon of paprika
- 2 teaspoon of curry spice
- 3 tablespoon of fresh lime juice
- ½ teaspoon of sea salt
- 1 teaspoon of freshly grated ginger
- 1 clove garlic, minced
- 2 pounds of large shrimp peeled and deveined

For the Sauce:

- 2 tablespoons of coconut oil or olive oil
- 1 small white onion, diced
- 2 teaspoons of freshly grated ginger
- 2 cloves garlic, minced
- 1 28 ounces can of diced tomatoes
- 3 tablespoons of red Thai curry paste
- 1 14 ounces coconut milk
- 1 teaspoon of sea salt
- 1/3 cup of freshly chopped cilantro for garnish (optional)

Cooking Instructions:

1. Make your marinade. In a medium bowl, add the coconut milk, spices, lime juice, sea salt, ginger, and garlic.

2. Whisk together and add the shrimp. Toss everything and allow to sit for a couple of minutes. Select the Sauté function on your Instant Pot.

3. When hot, add the oil. Add the onion, ginger, and garlic. Cook for a couple of minutes and press the Cancel function.

4. Add the tomatoes, curry paste, coconut milk, and salt. Secure the lid in place and ensure that the valve is in sealing position.

5. Select Manual High Pressure for 7 minutes. Do a quick pressure release and carefully remove the lid. Press the Cancel function.

6. Add the shrimp and the juices from the marinade. Simmer for about 4 minutes until the shrimp is cooked through and no longer pink.

7. Serve with optional cilantro, salt to taste, and over rice or cauliflower rice.

Crustless Crab Quiche

Preparation time: 15 minutes

Cooking time: 53 minutes

Total time: 1 hour 8 minutes

Calories: 380 kcal

Servings: 6

Ingredients:

- 1 tsp. sweet smoked paprika
- 5 eggs
- 1 cup half and half
- 10 oz. real crab meat, or a mix of crab and chopped raw shrimp
- 1 tsp. salt
- 1 tsp. pepper
- 1 tsp. Herbes de Provence
- 1 cup of shredded cheese
- 1 cup of chopped green onions green and white parts

Cooking Instructions:

1. Using a large bowl, mix together eggs and half-and-half with a whisk.

2. Put salt, pepper, sweet smoked paprika, Herbes de Provence, and shredded cheese, chopped green onions and stir with a fork to mix completely.

3. Put the real crab meat OR some combination of crab meat and chopped raw shrimp.

4. Spread out a sheet of aluminum foil that is cut bigger than the pan you want to use. Place the spring form pan on this sheet and crimp the sheet about the bottom.

5. Put the egg mixture into your spring form pan. Loosely close with foil or a silicone lid.

6. Put 2 cups of water into the inner pot of your Instant Pot and put a steamer rack in the pot. Put the covered spring form pan on the trivet.

7. Close and lock the lid in place and ensure that the valve is in sealing position. Press the manual key to cook on high pressure for about 50 minutes.

8. When the time is up, use a natural pressure release for about 10 minutes. Carefully remove the hot silicone pan.

9. With your knife, loosen the edges of the quiche from the pan. Remove the outer ring. Your dish is ready.

10. Serve and enjoy!

Coconut Fish Curry

Preparation time: 5 minutes

Cook time: 15 minutes

Total time: 20 minutes

Ingredients:

- 1-1.5 pound (500-750g) Fish steaks or fillets, rinsed and cut into bite-size pieces (fresh or frozen and thawed)
- 1 tomato, chopped
- 2 Green Chiles, sliced into strips
- 2 medium onions, sliced into strips
- 2 garlic cloves, squeezed
- 1 tablespoon of freshly grated Ginger, (or ⅛ tsp. of ginger powder)
- 6 curry leaves, or bay laurel leaves, or Kaffir lime leaves, or basil
- 1 tablespoon of ground coriander
- 2 teaspoons of ground cumin
- ½ teaspoon of ground turmeric
- 1 teaspoon of chili powder, or 1 teaspoon of Hot Pepper Flakes
- ½ teaspoon of ground Fenugreek (Methi)
- 3 tablespoons of curry powder mix
- 2 cups or (500ml) unsweetened coconut milk
- Salt to taste (we used about 2 teaspoons)
- Lemon juice to taste (we used the juice from ½ lemon)

Cooking Instructions:

1. Add a swirl of olive oil in your preheated Pressure Cooker on medium-low heat without the lid.

2. Place the curry leaves and lightly fry them for about 1 minute or until golden around the edges. Add the onion, garlic, and ginger.

3. Sauté the ingredients until the onion is soft. Add all of the ground spices like coriander, cumin, turmeric, chili powder and Fenugreek.

4. Cook the ingredients together with the onions for about 2 minutes or until they have released their aroma.

5. De-glaze with the coconut milk scraping up any browned bit stuck from the bottom of the pan. Add the green Chiles, tomatoes and fish pieces.

6. Give everything a good stir to coat the fish with the mixture. Secure the lid in place and ensure that the valve is in sealing position.

7. Set to cook on Low Pressure for 5 minutes. Do a natural pressure release for about 15 minutes.

8. Carefully open the lid and add more salt to taste and spritz with lemon juice.

9. Serve alone, or with steamed rice and enjoy!

Salmon with Chili-Lime Sauce

Preparation time: 7 minutes

Cooking time: 8 minutes

Total time: 15 minutes

Calories: 380 kcal

Servings: 3

Ingredients:

For steaming salmon:

- 1 tbsp. olive oil
- 2 cloves garlic minced
- 2 salmon fillets 5 oz. each
- 1 cup of water
- ½ tsp. paprika
- salt to taste
- Black pepper to taste (freshly ground)

For chili-lime sauce:

- 1 ½ lime juiced
- 1 １/２ tbsp. honey
- 1 tbsp. hot water
- 1 tbsp. chopped fresh parsley
- ½ tsp. cumin
- 1 jalapeno seeds removed and diced

Cooking Instructions:

1. Gather all the sauce ingredients and mix in a bowl and keep aside when done.

2. Put water to the pressure cooker and put salmon fillets on top of a steam rack inside the Instant Pot.

3. Add the salt and pepper to your taste on top of the salmon fillets and season.

4. Close and lock the lid in place and ensure that the valve is in sealing position.

5. Press the Manual button to cook on High Pressure for about 8 minutes.

6. When the time is up, use a natural pressure release for about 7 minutes.

7. Carefully open the lid once the pressure has been released and transfer the salmon to a serving plate.

8. Garnish with chili-lime sauce.

9. Serve and enjoy!

Clam Chowder

Preparation time: 13 minutes

Cook time: 17 minutes

Total time: 38 minutes

Servings: 4 - 6

Calories: 198 kcal

Ingredients:

- (3) 6.5 ounces cans chopped clams (set the clam juice aside)
- Water (to add to clam juice)
- 5 slices bacon, chopped
- 3 tablespoons of butter
- 1 onion, diced
- 2 stalks celery, diced
- 2 sprigs fresh thyme (or ¼ teaspoon of dried)
- 2 cloves garlic, pressed or finely minced
- 1 ¼ teaspoon of kosher salt (¾ teaspoon of table salt) or to taste
- ¼ teaspoon of pepper
- 1 ½ pounds of potatoes, 4 cups of diced (we used gold potatoes)
- ½ teaspoon of sugar (optional)
- 1/3 cups of half and half
- 1 tablespoon of potato or corn starch (optional, for thickening)
- Chopped chives, for garnish

Cooking Instructions:

1. First, open the cans of clams and drain the clam juice into a 2 cup measuring cup.

2. Add 2 cups of water and set the clams and juice water aside. Press the Sauté function and add the chopped bacon.

3. Cook, stirring occasionally, until fat is skimmed. Add the butter, onion, celery, and thyme. Scrape up any browned bit that stuck to the bottom of your pot.

4. Add the garlic, salt, and pepper. Cook for additional 1 minute, stirring frequently. Add the potatoes, sugar if desired and clam juice/water mixture.

5. Give everything a good stir. Secure the lid in place and ensure that the valve is in sealing position. Cancel the Sauté function.

6. Select Manual High Pressure for 4 minutes. Do a quick pressure release for about 3 minutes. Carefully remove the lid. Mash the potato with a potato masher.

7. Turn on the Sauté mode and set the lowest setting. Add the clams and the half and half. Allow the chowder to heat through.

8. Add a little bit potato or corn starch mixed with some of the hot chowder to thicken. Garnish with chopped chives.

9. Serve with crackers or some nice bread or rolls and enjoy!

PASTA
Cheesy Taco Pasta

Preparation time: 5 minutes

Cook time: 10 minutes

Total time: 15 minutes

Ingredients:

- 1 pound of ground beef
- Olive oil
- 5 cups of water
- ¾ of a 900g bag of large pasta shells
- 2 28g packages of taco seasoning
- 642ml jar of salsa (we used Pace's mild salsa)
- Shredded cheese
- Sour cream
- Green onions
- Tortilla chips (broken up)

Cooking Instructions:

1. Turn on the Sauté function on your Instant Pot and add the 1 pound of ground beef when it reads HOT.

2. Stir and break up your beef until browned. Add in your taco seasoning and give everything a good mix to coat the meat.

3. Add in your jar of salsa and water. Add the pasta shells and stir. Secure the lid in place and ensure that the valve is in sealing position.

4. Select Manual High Pressure for 10 minutes. Do a quick pressure release and carefully remove the lid. Give everything a good stir.

5. Serve with your desired toppings like shredded cheese, sour cream, green onions, and broken up tortilla chips!

Cheeseburger Macaroni

Preparation time: 15 minutes

Cook time: 3 minutes

Total time: 19 minutes

Servings: 5

Calories: 553 kcal

Ingredients:

- 1 cup of elbow macaroni uncooked
- 1 cup of water or can use chicken or beef broth
- 1 pound of ground beef or turkey
- 3 tablespoon of olive oil
- 1/3 onion diced (optional)
- 1 teaspoon of salt (optional)
- 1 teaspoon of garlic powder
- 1 can cheddar cheese soup
- ½ - 1 cup of sour cream
- 1 cup of cheddar cheese, shredded

Cooking Instructions:

1. Set your Instant Pot on Sauté setting and add the olive oil.

2. Add the ground beef and cook to brown. Add the diced onions and sauté until the ground beef is no longer pink. Press the Cancel function.

3. In a medium bowl, whisk together the water and cheddar cheese soup. Add the mixture on top of your ground beef. Add the uncooked noodles and do not stir.

4. Ensure that the noodles are completely submerged in the liquid. Secure the lid in place and ensure that the valve is in sealing position.

5. Select Manual High Pressure for 3 minutes. Do a natural pressure release and carefully open the lid. Select the Sauté function again.

6. Add the sour cream and shredded cheese. Gently stir and bring the pot to a boil to thicken for about 2 minutes.

7. Serve and enjoy!

Chicken Parmesan Casserole

Preparation time: 10 minutes

Cook time: 10 minutes

Total time: 20 minutes

Servings: 5

Calories: 392 kcal

Ingredients:

- 2 chicken breasts cut into chunks
- ½ onion diced
- 2 tablespoons of olive oil
- 1 teaspoon of salt to taste
- 1 teaspoon of basil
- 1 jar spaghetti sauce 24 ounces
- 2 cups of water
- 2 cups of noodles uncooked, small shapes of your choice
- 1 teaspoon of garlic, minced
- 2 tablespoons of butter
- 1/3 cup of bread crumbs
- 1 cup of parmesan cheese

Cooking Instructions:

1. Set your Instant Pot on Sauté, normal function and add the olive oil.

2. Add the chicken cut up into bite size pieces. Sauté for about 2 minutes to brown. Add the diced onions and garlic.

3. Cook the chicken for additional 3 minutes or until chicken pieces are about half way done. Add the salt, basil, spaghetti sauce, water, and give everything a good stir.

4. Add 2 cups of uncooked noodles. Place the noodles down to submerge under the sauce and do not stir. Secure the lid in place. Select Manual High Pressure for 10 minutes.

5. Do a quick pressure release and carefully remove the lid. Stir in 2/3 cup of grated parmesan.

6. In a medium bowl, melt your butter and stir in 1/3 cup of bread crumbs and 1/3 cup of grated parmesan.

7. Sprinkle the bread crumb mixture on top and serve immediately.

Cheesy Chicken & Pasta

Preparation time: 5 minutes

Cook time: 19 minutes

Total time: 24 minutes

Serves: 8

Ingredients:

- 2 lb. of skinless boneless chicken breasts cut into 1-inch
- 1 tbsp. of EVOO
- 4 tbsp. of salted butter
- 1 bag/box (16 oz.) orecchiette pasta.
- 1 ¼ cups of heavy cream
- 2 cups of warm-hot water
- 1 tbsp. of yellow mustard
- 1 tsp. of sea salt
- ½ tsp. of black pepper
- 3 cups of shredded mild cheddar cheese
- ¼ cup of parmesan cheese

Cooking Instructions:

1. Press the Sauté function and add in olive oil.

2. Add the 1-inch cubed chicken chunks when it reads HOT. Sauté the chicken for about 4-5 minutes.

3. Add the rest of the ingredients except the heavy cream and cheeses. Secure the lid in place and ensure that the valve is in sealing position.

4. Mix the pasta with the chicken and liquid in your Instant Pot. Select Manual High Pressure for 12 minutes.

5. Do a natural pressure release for about 5 minutes, then quick release the remaining pressure. Carefully open the lid and Press the Sauté setting.

6. Add in heavy cream, parmesan cheese, and shredded cheese. Stir in pasta and cheese mixture until all cheese has melted.

7. Turn off your Instant Pot and let the pasta sit for about 3 to 4 minutes before serving. Serve and enjoy!

Vegetable Noodle Soup

Preparation time: 10 minutes

Cook time: 11 minutes

Total time: 21 minutes

Servings: 4

Ingredients:

- 1 onion, finely chopped
- 1 large carrot, diced
- ½ small sweet potato, diced
- 1 clove of garlic, crushed
- ½ cup of frozen sweetcorn
- 1 tablespoon of tomato paste
- 1 teaspoon of paprika
- ¼ teaspoon of garlic powder
- ¼ teaspoon of Chili powder
- A pinch of dried basil, oregano, thyme and parsley
- Salt and black pepper
- 5 cups (1.2 liters) of vegetable or chicken stock
- 100g (3.5 ounces) of uncooked pasta of choice
- 4 handfuls of spinach
- Spraying oil

Cooking Instructions:

1. Press the Sauté function on your Instant Pot.

2. Once hot, spray with spray oil, add onion, garlic and carrots and sauté for about 2 minutes to soften.

3. Mix in the sweet potato, tomato paste and spices and herbs and give everything a good stir to coat. Add the stock, sweetcorn and pasta.

4. Secure the lid in place. Select Manual High Pressure for 8 minutes. Do a quick pressure release and carefully open the lid.

5. Stir through the spinach. Season with salt and black pepper to taste. Top with a little grated parmesan if desired.

6. Serve and enjoy!

Chicken, Spinach, and Artichoke Pasta

Preparation time: 10 minutes

Cook time: 3 minutes

Total time: 13 minutes

Ingredients:

- 1-1.5 pounds of boneless skinless chicken breast cubed
- 2 tablespoons of minced garlic
- 1 tablespoon of olive oil
- 2 cups of chicken broth
- 1 cup of water
- 12 ounces of penne pasta
- ¾ cup of light cream
- 6 ounces of pesto
- 14 ounces can quartered artichoke hearts in water drained and chopped
- ½ cup of shredded parmesan cheese
- 1 cup of baby spinach

Cooking Instructions:

1. Set your Instant Pot to Sauté function and add the garlic when it reads HOT.

2. Sauté the garlic for 1 minute or so until it turns brown. Add the chicken breast. Season with salt and pepper to taste.

3. Cook the chicken for about 2 to 3 minutes or until the sides start to brown. Turn off the Instant Pot and add the pasta, broth, and water.

4. Secure the lid in place and ensure that the valve is in sealing position. Select Manual High Pressure for 3 minutes.

5. Do a quick pressure release when the timer beeps. Turn on the Instant Pot on Sauté setting and add pesto and artichokes.

6. Cook for 1 minute and add the cream and cheese. Cook for additional 1 minute and turn off your Instant Pot. Add the spinach and give everything a good stir until wilted.

7. Serve immediately and enjoy!

Lasagna Casserole

Preparation time: 10 minutes

Cook time: 10 minutes

Total time: 20 minutes

Calories: 584 kcal

Ingredients:

- 2 cups of water
- 2 cups of pasta uncooked, we use Barilla penne pasta
- 1 cup of ricotta cheese we use Galbani
- 2 cups of mozzarella cheese we use Galbani with whole milk
- 1 jar spaghetti sauce 25.5 ounces, I used Barilla Traditional
- 1 teaspoon of garlic salt
- ½ teaspoon of basil
- ¼ teaspoon of white pepper
- 1 pound of ground beef
- 2 tablespoons of olive oil
- 1 small onion, diced
- 1 can diced tomatoes optional

Cooking Instructions:

1. Press the Sauté function on your Instant Pot and add the olive oil. Add the onions and cook until browned.

2. Add the ground beef and sauté for a couple of minutes or until they are no longer pink. Drain grease.

3. Transfer back into your Instant Pot for some minutes with onions and spices. Cook the contents until beef is done and onions soften.

4. Turn off the Instant Pot. Ensure that the ground beef mixture evenly spread on the bottom of your Instant Pot.

5. Add the spaghetti sauce, water and uncooked noodles. Do not stir and slowly push down the noodles to submerge in the liquid. Secure the lid.

6. Select Manual High Pressure for 5 minutes. Do a natural pressure release and carefully open the lid.

7. Stir in ½ cup of ricotta cheese and 1.5 cup of mozzarella cheese and top with a dollop of ricotta. Give everything a good stir until cheese is melted.

8. Serve with a dollop of ricotta and mozzarella on top if desired and enjoy.

Pizza Pasta

Preparation time: 5 minutes

Cook time: 3 minutes

Total time: 10 minutes

Servings: 6

Calories: 303 kcal

Ingredients:

- 4 cups of noodles (I used ziti or riganoti)
- 8 cups of water
- 1 ½ cup of mozzarella cheese, shredded
- 2 cups of spaghetti sauce
- 10 pepperoni cut in half
- 6 mushrooms, quartered (optional)

Cooking Instructions:

1. Add the noodles and water into the bottom of your Instant Pot.

2. Secure the lid in place and ensure that the valve is in sealing position. Select Manual High Pressure for 3 minutes.

3. Do a quick pressure release and carefully open the lid. Turn off your Instant Pot and drain the water.

4. Transfer the pasta back into your Instant Pot. Add the shredded cheese, spaghetti sauce and sliced pepperoni.

5. Give everything a good stir. Press the Sauté function and allow the sauce to bubbles and cheese melts a bit.

6. Serve and enjoy!

Macaroni and Cheese

Preparation time: 5 minutes

Cook time: 3 minutes

Total time: 16 minutes

Servings: 4

Calories: 649 kcal

Ingredients:

- 3 cups of noodles macaroni
- 4 cups of water
- ¾ - 1 cup of evaporated milk 1 cup
- 3 cups of cheese can use more of course
- 3 tablespoons of butter

Cooking Instructions:

1. Pour the water into the bottom of your Instant Pot.

2. Add the macaroni noodles, and salt. Secure the lid in place and ensure that the valve is in sealing position.

3. Select Manual High Pressure for 2 minutes. Do a quick pressure release when timer beeps and carefully remove the lid. Drain the remaining water.

4. Set your Instant Pot to Low and add the butter to melt. Add the evaporated milk and 3 cups of cheese.

5. Cook, stirring until all cheese is melted and your macaroni and cheese has achieved your desired consistency.

6. Turn off your Instant Pot. Allow the pot to sit for a couple of minutes to be thicker before serving.

7. Serve and enjoy!

Chicken Fajita Pasta

Preparation time: 5 minutes

Cook time: 5 minutes

Total time: 10 minutes

Ingredients:

- 1 pound of boneless skinless chicken breasts, towel dried, and cut into bite-size portions
- 3 tablespoons of fajita seasoning (homemade or store bought packet), divided in half
- 4 tablespoons of olive oil, divided
- 1 medium onion, diced
- 2 bell peppers, seeded and diced
- 5 cloves fresh garlic, minced
- 2½ cups low sodium chicken broth
- 1 can (10 ounces) fire-roasted tomatoes with juices
- 8 ounces dry penne pasta
- Freshly ground black pepper, to taste

Cooking Instructions:

1. Press the Sauté function and adjust to More for high heat.

2. When it says HOT, add 2 tablespoons of oil. Add the chicken and half the seasoning and toss everything to coat.

3. Cook the chicken until white. Add the onions, bell peppers, and garlic, along with rest of the seasoning.

4. Cook, stirring until the veggies are slightly tender for about 2 minutes. Add the broth, tomatoes with all its juices, and dry pasta into your Instant Pot.

5. Secure the lid in place. Select Manual High Pressure for 5 minutes. Do a quick pressure release and carefully open the lid.

6. Add the freshly ground black pepper to taste. Give everything a good stir to combine.

7. Serve and enjoy!

Tuna Noodle Casserole

Preparation time: 10 minutes

Cook time: 3 minutes

Total time: 13 minutes

Servings: 6

Calories: 454 kcal

Ingredients:

- 12 ounces egg noodles
- 1 can tuna 8-12 ounces albacore chunk preferred, drained
- 1 cup of frozen peas
- 1 cup of mushrooms, sliced
- 3 cup of chicken broth
- 1 teaspoon of salt
- 1 teaspoon of garlic powder
- ½ teaspoon of pepper (optional)
- 1 cup half and half
- 1.5 cup of cheese

Cooking Instructions:

1. Add all ingredients except for half and half and cheese into the bottom of your Instant Pot.

2. Slowly stir everything together. Secure the lid in place and ensure that the valve is in sealing position. Select Manual High Pressure for 3 minutes.

3. Do a quick pressure release and carefully open the lid. Gently stir in half and half and cheese until cheese is melted.

4. Let it sit for about 5 minutes to thicken bit. In a medium bowl, add some hot liquid with some cornstarch and add them back into the pot to thicken quicker.

5. Serve and enjoy!

Cauliflower and Pasta Alfredo

Serves: 6

Preparation time: 5 minutes

Cook time: 20 minutes

Total time: 25 minutes

Ingredients:

- 1 head cauliflower, stem and leaves removed
- 2 tablespoons of butter
- 4 cloves garlic, minced
- 1 cup of chicken broth
- ¼ cup of half and half
- 1 teaspoon of onion powder
- 2 teaspoons of garlic powder
- 1 teaspoon of salt, or more to taste
- 1 box fettuccini noodles
- Sun dried tomatoes or/and green onions for garnish (optional)

Cooking Instructions:

1. Turn on the Sauté function and add the butter when it reads HOT.

2. Add the garlic and cook until garlic is softened. Add the 1 cup of chicken broth, and the head of cauliflower into the bottom of your Instant Pot.

3. Secure the lid in place and ensure that the valve is in sealing position. Select Manual High Pressure for 6 minutes.

4. Bring a pot of water to boil on the stovetop and add the fettuccine in the water to boil just until done. Drain water and reserve aside.

5. Do a natural pressure release for about 10 minutes, then quick release any remaining pressure. Blend the cauliflower with your immersion blender until pureed.

6. Add the onion powder, garlic powder and salt, and puree until a smooth sauce. Add ¼ - ½ cup of half and half to thicken.

7. Serve with pasta and garnish with chopped onions and sun dried tomatoes.

BEANS, RICE & GRAINS
Mexican Green Rice

Preparation time: 10 minutes

Cook time: 8 minutes

Servings: 10

Calories: 232 kcal

Ingredients:

- 3 ½ cups of water or chicken stock
- 1 cup of tightly packed fresh cilantro leaves
- 1 large Poblano chili, seeded and roughly chopped
- 1 green onion, cut into pieces
- 2 garlic cloves
- 3 cups of long grain white rice
- 2 tbsp. of canola or vegetable oil
- Salt to taste, if needed
- ¼ tsp. of cumin
- 1 tsp. of white vinegar
- 2-3 tbsp. of fresh lime juice

Cooking Instructions:

1. Blend in a blender water, cilantro, poblano, green onion and garlic until well blend and smooth.

2. Add the rice in a fine mesh colander and place it under cold running water to rinse until the water runs clear.

3. Press the "Sauté" function on your Instant Pot and adjust to more. When hot, add the oil. Add the rinsed rice.

4. Toast the rice for about 3 minutes or until some of the moisture is absorbed and rice appears a little toasted and coated with oil, stirring constantly.

5. Add the water and cilantro mixture, salt, cumin, vinegar and give everything a good stir to combine. Bring the pot to a boil.

6. Secure the lid in place and ensure that the valve is in sealing position. Select Manual High Pressure for 8 minutes.

7. Do a natural pressure release for about 5 minutes, then quick release the remaining pressure. Carefully open the lid and give everything a good stir.

8. Sprinkle lime juice over the cooked rice. Fluff rice with a fork and serve immediately.

New Orleans-Style Red Beans and Rice

Preparation time: 10 minutes

Cook time: 50 minutes

Total time: 1 hour

Yield: 6-8

Ingredients:

- 1 tbsp. of oil
- 1 lb. smoked sausage, sliced
- ¼ stick of butter
- 2 cups of chopped seasoning blend (onions, celery, green bell peppers, parsley flakes)
- 1 clove garlic, chopped
- 1 (1 lb.) package Camellia Brand Red Kidney Beans
- 6 cups of water
- 1 bay leaf
- Salt and pepper to taste
- Cajun seasoning to taste
- Hot cooked rice

Cooking Instruction:

1. Rinse and sort the beans. Turn on your Instant Pot and select the Sauté function.

2. When hot, add the oil. Add the sliced sausage, and cook for about 5 minutes or until browned. Remove the sausage to a paper towel-lined plate and set aside.

3. Add the ¼ stick of butter into the bottom of your Instant Pot along with chopped seasoning blend and garlic. Cook the ingredients until onions turn soft.

4. Transfer the cooked sausage back to your Instant Pot along with the beans, water, and bay leaf. Give everything a good stir. Turn off the Sauté function.

5. Secure the lid in place and ensure that the valve is in sealing position. Select Manual High Pressure for 40 minutes. Do a natural pressure release for about 20 minutes.

6. Carefully open the lid. Mash the beans with a potato masher to your desired creamy consistency. Add salt, pepper, and Cajun seasoning to taste. Serve hot and enjoy!

13 Bean Soup

Preparation time: 6 minutes

Cooking time: 15 minutes

Total time: 21 minutes

Servings: 4

Ingredients:

- 1 cup of carrots chopped
- 1 ham bone
- 1 big diced tomato
- 2 cups of celery minced
- 2 tsp. chili powder
- 1 tsp. garlic powder
- 1 tsp. sea salt
- 1 big diced tomato
- 1 big diced tomato
- ¼ tsp. pepper
- 2 cups of 13 bean soup consisting of various beans, lentils, peas

Cooking Instructions:

1. Put your beans in the Instant Pot and put 3 ½ cups of water.

2. Close and lock the lid in place and ensure that the valve is in sealing position. Select Manual function to cook on High Pressure for 15 minutes.

3. When the time is up, use a natural pressure release for about 8-10 minutes. Carefully rinse and drain the beans, put the beans back into the Instant Pot and add the ham bone.

5. Put enough water and cook, setting the cooker with a natural pressure release. Remove the ham bone and add all the ingredients. Close and lock the lid in place and ensure that the valve is in sealing position.

6. Press the manual key to cook on high pressure for about 15 minutes. When the time is up, use a natural pressure release for about 20 minutes.

7. Serve and enjoy!

Baked Beans

Preparation time: 7 minutes

Cooking time: 40 minutes

Total time: 47 minutes

Servings: 6

Ingredients:

- 3 cloves garlic, diced
- 1 tsp. sea salt
- 2 lbs. small white beans
- 1 tbsp. mustard powder
- 1 big onion, minced
- 1 cup molasses
- 1/2 cup of maple syrup
- ¼ tsp. ground pepper
- 5 cups of water
- 2 cups of balsamic vinegar

Cooking Instructions:

1. Add the beans with 2 or 3 cups water into the bottom of your Instant Pot and cook on high pressure for 10 minutes.

4. Rinse and drain the water out then place them back into the Instant Pot. Pour enough water and put all the ingredients.

5. Close and lock the lid in place and ensure that the valve is in sealing position. Press the manual function to cook on high pressure for about 40 minutes.

6. When the time is up, use a natural pressure release for about 25 minutes. Cook on bean setting for 40 minutes and release natural pressure.

7. Carefully open the lid and remove the pan from your Instant Pot.

8. Serve and enjoy!

Red Beans and Rice

Preparation time: 10 minutes

Cook time: 12 minutes

Total time: 22 minutes

Calories: 560 kcal

Ingredients:

- ¼ onion, diced
- 6 strips bacon, diced
- 1 tablespoon of garlic, minced
- 2-3 tablespoons of olive oil
- 12 ounces Andouille sausage precooked, dice
- 1 can of red beans drained ☐ 2 cups of rice uncooked
- 2 ½ cups of chicken broth
- 2 cups of water
- 1 teaspoon of cumin
- 1 teaspoon salt

Cooking Instructions:

1. Set your Instant Pot on Sauté setting and adjust to high.

2. When hot, add the olive oil. Add the onions, garlic and bacon and sauté until the bacon and onions soften.

3. Add the precooked sausage. Press the Cancel function to turn off your Instant Pot. Add the red beans, drained and rinsed.

4. Add the chicken broth and water. Add the uncooked rice, salt, and cumin. Give everything a good stir.

5. Secure the lid in place and ensure that the valve is in sealing position. Select the Rice function and set for 12 minutes.

6. Do a quick pressure release and carefully remove the lid. Give everything a good stir.

7. Serve and enjoy!

Rice Pudding

Preparation time: 5 minutes

Cook time: 14 minutes

Total time: 19 minutes

Servings: 5

Calories: 198 kcal

Ingredients:

- 1 cup of uncooked rice
- ½ cup of sugar
- 1 cup of water
- 1 tablespoon of butter
- 2 cups of milk 2% or whole is best
- 1 egg
- ¼ cup of evaporated milk
- ½ teaspoon of vanilla
- ½ teaspoon of almond extract (optional)
- A pinch of nutmeg (optional)
- A pinch of cinnamon (optional)

Cooking Instructions:

1. Set your Instant Pot on Sauté function and add butter until melted.

2. Add rice and give everything a good stir to coat. Add the milk, water, vanilla, cinnamon, almond extract if desired and sugar.

3. Give everything a good stir to combine. Secure the lid in place and ensure that the valve is in sealing position. Select Manual High Pressure for 14 minutes.

4. Do a natural pressure release and carefully open the lid. In a medium bowl, whisk together the egg and evaporated milk.

5. Spoon a spoonful of rice pudding mixture into egg mixture and stir. Add another warm spoonful of rice mixture and give everything a good stir.

6. Place a bowl full of egg mixture into the bottom of your Instant Pot and select the Sauté function. Allow to get hot and bubbles for about 30-60 seconds to thicken.

7. Serve warm or chilled, top with cinnamon or nutmeg.

Mexican Rice & Beans

Preparation time: 5 minutes

Cook time: 35 minutes

Total time: 1 hour

Servings: 8

Calories: 285 kcal

Ingredients:

- ½ tbsp. of avocado oil
- 1 onion, diced
- 1 yellow or red pepper, diced
- 1 tsp. of minced garlic
- 2 cups of short grain brown rice
- 1 cup of dried red beans
- 1 cup of salsa
- 1 tbsp. of taco seasoning
- 5 cups of vegetable or chicken stock
- Cheese, sour cream, cilantro for serving

Cooking Instructions:

1. Set your Instant Pot to Sauté setting and adjust to High.

2. When hot, add in oil, onions, and peppers and cook for about for 2 to 3 minutes to soften. Add in garlic and cook for additional 1 minute.

3. Add in rice, beans, salsa, seasonings and stock. Give everything a good stir. Secure the lid in place and ensure that the valve is in sealing position.

4. Cancel the Sauté function. Select Manual High Pressure for 35 minutes. Do a natural pressure release for about 15 minutes.

5. Serve with your desired toppings and enjoy!

Pinto Beans & Ham Hocks

Serves: 6

Preparation time: 10 minutes

Cook time: 40 minutes

Total time: 50 minutes

Ingredients:

- 1 (1 lb.) package Camellia Brand Pinto Beans
- 1 large smoked ham hock
- 1 large yellow onion, finely chopped
- 2 large cloves garlic, minced
- 2 dried red chile peppers, or ¼ tsp. of red chile flakes
- ¾ tsp. of salt
- ¼ tsp. of freshly ground black pepper
- 6 cups of water or chicken broth
- 1 bunch green onions, chopped

Cooking Instructions:

1. Rinse and sort the beans.

2. Add the beans and ham hock into the bottom of your Instant Pot. Add the onion, chilies, salt, pepper, and water or broth.

3. Secure the lid in place and ensure that the valve is in sealing position. Select Manual High Pressure for 40 minutes.

4. Do a natural pressure release for about 20 minutes. Carefully open the lid and remove ham hocks with tongs. Discard skin, bones and cartilage.

5. Shred the ham and transfer them back into beans. Give everything a good stir.

6. Serve sprinkled with green onions and enjoy!

Spanish Rice with Black Beans and Potatoes

Serves: 4-6

Preparation time: 10 minutes

Cook time: 22 minutes

Total time: 32 minutes

Ingredients:

- 2 cups of brown rice, washed
- 4 cups of water
- 1 14.5 ounces can no salt added diced tomatoes
- 3 small potatoes, cubed
- 1 teaspoon of cumin powder
- ½ teaspoon of garlic powder
- ½ teaspoon of coriander powder
- 1 teaspoon of turmeric
- ½ teaspoon of smoked paprika
- Salt and pepper to taste
- 1 15 ounces can black beans rinsed and drained

Cooking Instructions:

1. Add all ingredients, except black beans, into the bottom of your Instant Pot.

2. Secure the lid in place and ensure that the valve is in sealing position.

3. Select Manual High Pressure for 22 minutes.

4. Do a natural pressure release for about 10 minutes, then quick release the remaining pressure.

5. Carefully remove the lid and stir in the black beans.

6. Scoop into bowls and serve immediately.

Pinto Beans

Preparation time: 5 minutes

Cooking time: 30 minutes

Total time: 35 minutes

Servings: 5

Ingredients:

- 1 1/2 cup pinto beans, selected and washed
- 3 cups of filtered water
- 1 medium onion
- 1 jalapeno, diced
- 1 tbsp. sea salt
- ¼ cup avocado oil
- 1 bay leaf
- 2 cloves garlic, chopped

Cooking Instructions:

1. Put beans, water, bay leaf and garlic into the bottom of your Instant Pot.

2. Close and lock the lid in place and ensure that the valve is in sealing position.

3. Select Manual function to cook on high pressure for 30 minutes. When the time is up, use a natural pressure release.

4. Turn the beans and water into a big container and set the Instant Pot to sauté mode. Sauté the onion and jalapeno in the olive oil and put the sea salt.

5. Put the beans and water back into the Instant Pot using the same settings. Mix thoroughly the beans and cook until your refried beans are thickened.

6. When the time is up, use a natural pressure release for about 25 minutes. Carefully open the lid once the pressure has been released.

7. Serve and enjoy!

Black Beans

Preparation time: 7 minutes

Cook time: 25 minutes

Total time: 32 minutes

Servings: 6

Calories: 104 kcal

Ingredients:

- 450g / 2½ cups of dried black beans, no need to soak before using
- 1 medium onion, chopped finely
- 4 cloves garlic, chopped finely
- 1 tsp. of chili flakes, or 1 fresh chili
- 1 tbsp. of ground cumin
- 1 tsp. of ground coriander
- 1 large bay leaf
- 1 tsp. of dried mint, (optional)
- 720 mls / 3 cups flavorful broth/stock
- 1 lime, juice only
- 1 tsp. of salt, or more to taste

Cooking Instructions:

1. Place all ingredients except the lime into the bottom of your Instant Pot.

2. Give everything a good stir. Secure the lid in place and ensure that the valve is in sealing position.

3. Select Manual High Pressure for 25 minutes. Do a natural pressure release and carefully remove the lid.

4. Add salt to taste and squeeze the juice of the lime into the beans. Give everything a good stir to combine.

5. Serve immediately and enjoy!

VEGAN & VEGETARIAN

Cilantro Lime Quinoa

Preparation time: 6 minutes

Cooking time: 10 minutes

Total time: 16 minutes

Calories: 97 kcal

Servings: 5

Ingredients:

- 2 tbsp. lime juice
- 1 cup of quinoa rinsed and drained (any color)
- Salt to taste
- Zest of one lime
- ½ cup of chopped cilantro
- 1 ¼ cups of vegetable broth

Cooking Instructions:

1. Put the quinoa and 1 ¼ cup vegetable broth to the Instant Pot.

2. Close and lock the lid in place and ensure that the valve is in sealing position.

3. Press the Manual key to cook on High Pressure for about 5 minutes.

4. When the time is up, use a natural pressure release for about 7 minutes.

5. Carefully open the lid and pour the lime juice, lime zest, and cilantro. Taste and add salt to taste.

6. Serve and enjoy!

Vegan Lentil Chili

Preparation time: 10 minutes

Cooking time: 22 minutes

Total time: 32 minutes

Servings: 5

Ingredients:

- 1 tsp. dried oregano
- 1 onion, chopped
- 4 cloves minced garlic
- 2 carrots, chopped
- 2 jalapeños, chopped
- 1 ½ tbsp. chili powder
- ½ tsp. ground coriander
- ½ tsp. salt
- ½ cup of chopped fresh cilantro
- 1 14 oz. can crushed tomatoes
- 1 30 oz. can fire roasted diced tomatoes
- 1 tbsp. olive oil
- 2 cups of brown or green lentils.
- 4 ½ cups of vegetable broth
- 1 tsp. fresh lime juice
- 1 tbsp. cumin

Cooking Instructions:

1. Add the olive oil in the Instant Pot, hit the sauté button on the Instant Pot and heat the oil for sometimes.

2. Add the onion, garlic, carrots and jalapeños and heat until soft, about 4 minutes. Add the spices and remaining ingredients except for lime juice and cilantro.

3. Close and lock the lid in place and ensure that the valve is in sealing position. Press the Manual function to cook on High Pressure for about 15 minutes.

4. When the time is up, use a natural pressure release for about 10 minutes. Carefully open the lid once the pressure has been released. Pour lime juice and cilantro.

5. Serve immediately and enjoy!

Quinoa Burrito Bowls

Preparation time: 5 minutes

Cook time: 20 minutes

Total time: 25 minutes

Servings: 4

Calories: 163 kcal

Ingredients:

- 1 tsp. of extra-virgin olive oil
- ½ red onion, diced
- 1 bell pepper, diced
- ½ tsp. of salt
- 1 tsp. of ground cumin
- 1 cup of quinoa, rinsed well
- 1 cup of prepared salsa
- 1 cup of water
- 1 ½ cups cooked black beans, or 1 (15 ounces) can, drained and rinsed
- Optional toppings: Avocado, guacamole, fresh cilantro, green onions, salsa, lime wedges, shredded lettuce

Cooking Instructions:

1. Set your Instant Pot to Sauté function and heat the oil.

2. Sauté the onions and peppers for about 6 minutes or until the onion begin to soften.

3. Add in cumin and salt and cook for additional 1 minute. Turn off your Instant Pot. Add in the quinoa, salsa, water, and beans.

4. Secure the lid in place and ensure that the valve is in sealing position. Select the "Rice" function to cook on Low Pressure for 12 minutes.

5. Do a natural pressure release for about 15 minutes. Carefully open the lid and fluff the quinoa with a fork.

6. Serve warm, with your desired toppings like avocado, diced onions, salsa, and shredded lettuce.

Walnut Lentil Tacos

Preparation time: 5 minutes

Cooking time: 10 minutes

Total time: 15 minutes

Yield: 11-12 tacos

Ingredients:

- ½ tsp. garlic powder
- 1 white onion, diced
- 1 ½ tbsp. olive oil
- 1 cup of dried brown lentils
- 2 garlic clove, minced
- 1 tbsp. chili powder
- ¼ tsp. onion powder
- 1/3 tsp. red pepper flakes
- 1 ½ tsp. ground cumin
- ½ tsp. kosher salt
- 1/3 tsp. freshly ground pepper
- 2 ½ cups of vegetable broth
- 1/2 tsp. paprika
- 1 14 oz. can fire-roasted diced tomatoes
- ¾ cup of chopped walnuts
- 1/3 tsp. oregano

Taco toppings of choice: shredded lettuce, tomato, jalapenos, flour or corn tortillas

Cooking Instructions:

1. Switch the Instant Pot on and press the Sauté button.

2. Add the olive oil, onion and garlic clove and sauté until onion cooked through and stir occasionally for about 4 minutes.

3. Add the spices and stir together. Press cancel and put the vegetable broth, tomatoes, walnuts and lentils and stir to mix well.

4. Close and lock the lid in place and ensure that the valve is in sealing position.

5. Press the Manual button to cook on High Pressure for about 10 minutes.

6. When the time is up, use a natural pressure release for about 4 minutes.

7. Carefully open the lid and stir lentils, seasoning to taste if needed.

8. You may add toppings of your choice.

9. Serve immediately and enjoy!

Buttery Garlic Mashed Potatoes

Preparation time: 6 minutes

Cook time: 6 minutes

Total time: 12 minutes

Ingredients:

- 3 pounds (1.5kg) red and Yukon Gold potatoes, peeled if desired, halved or quartered
- 4 garlic cloves, peeled
- 1 ½ cups (375ml) low sodium chicken stock
- 3 tbsp. of butter or ghee, plus more for serving
- ¾ cup of heavy cream
- Salt and freshly ground black pepper
- Minced fresh thyme, for garnish (optional)

Cooking Instructions:

1. Add the potatoes, garlic, salt, black pepper, chicken stock, and butter or ghee into the bottom of your Instant Pot.

2. Secure the lid in place and ensure that the valve is in sealing position. Select Manual High Pressure for 6 minutes.

3. Do a quick pressure release and carefully open the lid. Mash the potatoes right in the pot with a potato masher.

4. Add the heavy cream, and mash until your desired consistency is achieved. Adjust the seasoning with more salt and pepper.

5. Serve warm, topped with additional butter or ghee and fresh thyme.

Mushroom Risotto

Preparation time: 12 minutes

Cooking time: 20 minutes

Total time: 32 minutes

Calories: 370 kcal

Servings: 5

Ingredients:

- 1 ½ tbsp. olive oil
- 2 ½ tbsp. vegan butter, divided
- 1 medium onion, diced
- 4 cloves garlic, minced
- 10 oz. cremini mushrooms dry brushed & minced
- ¾ tsp. dried thyme
- 1 ½ cups of Arborio rice
- ½ cup of dry white wine
- 4 cups of vegetable broth, low sodium
- 1 ¼ tsp. sea salt, more to taste
- Fresh ground pepper to taste
- 1 cup of frozen peas, thawed
- 4 tbsp. Vegan Parmesan Cheese (optional)

Cooking Instructions:

1. Switch on the Sauté mode of your Instant Pot and put the oil and butter. Heat the oil; put the onions and sauté about 3 minutes.

2. Add the garlic and thyme and sauté for a minute. Add the mushrooms and sauté for about 4 minutes until soft.

3. Add the rice and stir to coat well. Pour the wine and cook until the liquid mostly cooks down. About 2 minutes. Put the broth, salt, and pepper.

4. Close and lock the lid in place and ensure that the valve is in sealing position. Press the Manual setting to cook on High Pressure for about 6 minutes.

5. When the time is up, use a natural pressure release for about 6 minutes. Note the risotto will look soupy when you first remove the lid.

6. Just stir for sometimes and it will thicken up. Add the peas, butter, and vegan parmesan. If you need some seasoning, you may add it.

7. Top with fresh-cut parsley, crushed red pepper flakes, and fresh cracked pepper.

8. Serve and enjoy!

Lentil Curry

Serving: 3 cups

Preparation time: 10 minutes

Cook time: 15 minutes

Total time: 45 minutes

Ingredients:

- 1 ½ cups of green or brown lentils
- ½ tbsp. of coconut oil
- 1 small shallot, finely chopped
- 3 tbsp. of minced fresh ginger
- 2 tbsp. of minced garlic (about 6 cloves)
- 1 tbsp. of plus 1 tsp. of curry powder
- ½ tbsp. of coconut sugar or brown sugar
- 1 tsp. of kosher salt
- ¾ tsp. of ground turmeric
- 1/8 - ¼ tsp. of cayenne pepper
- 1 (14 oz.) can light coconut milk
- 2 tbsp. of freshly squeezed lemon juice (about ½ large lemon)
- Cooked brown rice, for serving
- Chopped fresh cilantro, for serving

Cooking Instructions:

1. Rinse and drain the lentils, then set aside. Press the Sauté function on your Instant Pot and add the coconut oil.

2. When melted, add 1 tbsp. of water, the shallot, ginger, and garlic. Sauté for about 2 minutes, stirring often until very fragrant and the shallot is soft.

3. Add the curry powder, coconut sugar, salt, turmeric, and cayenne. Give everything a good stir. Add the lentils, coconut milk, and 1 cup of water.

4. Stir to coat the lentils completely with the liquid. Select the Cancel function to stop the Sauté mode. Secure the lid in place.

5. Select Manual High Pressure for 15 minutes. Do a natural pressure release and carefully remove the lid. Stir in the lemon juice. Add more seasoning to taste.

6. Serve warm with rice, sprinkled with cilantro.

Pasta Rigatoni Bolognese

Preparation time: 5 minutes

Cook time: 20 minutes

Total time: 25 minutes

Servings: 6

Ingredients:

- 3 tablespoons of olive oil
- ½ cup onion, finely chopped
- ½ cup celery, finely chopped
- ½ cup carrots, finely chopped
- ½ cup bell peppers, finely chopped
- 1 tablespoon of garlic, minced
- 2 cups of fresh mushrooms, chopped
- 1 cup of water
- 1 ounces dried porcini mushrooms, chopped
- 1 (28 ounces) can crushed tomatoes
- ½ teaspoon of black pepper
- 1 teaspoon of salt (or to taste)
- ¼ teaspoon of dried thyme
- 1 teaspoon of dried oregano
- 1 teaspoon of dried basil
- 1 teaspoon of sugar
- 1 tablespoon of balsamic vinegar
- 1 tablespoon of tomato paste
- ½ teaspoon of crushed red pepper flakes (or to taste)
- 12 ounces rigatoni pasta
- 1 cup of whole milk
- 1 cup of red wine
- 4 ounces mascarpone cheese
- ¼ cup of parmesan cheese, finely grated
- 3 tablespoons of fresh parsley, chopped

Cooking Instructions:

1. Set your Instant Pot to 'Sauté' function and add olive oil.

2. Add the onions, celery, carrots, bell peppers and garlic and cook for about 3 minutes, stirring frequently.

3. Add the fresh mushrooms and cook for 2 minutes. Press Cancel to turn off the Instant Pot.

4. Deglaze the pot with 2 tablespoons of water to remove any browned bit stuck to the bottom of the pot.

5. Add in dried porcini mushrooms, crushed tomatoes, black pepper, salt, thyme, oregano, basil, sugar, balsamic vinegar, tomato paste, crushed red pepper, pasta, milk, wine and water.

6. Give everything a good stir to combine. Secure the lid and ensure that the valve is in sealing position. Select Manual High Pressure for 7 minutes.

7. Do a quick pressure release and carefully open the lid. Stir in mascarpone cheese. Allow the pasta to rest for a couple of minutes to thicken up before serving.

8. Sprinkle with Parmesan and fresh parsley and serve immediately.

Maple Bourbon Sweet Potato Chili

Preparation time: 10 minutes

Cooking time: 23 minutes

Total time: 33 minutes

Calories: 220 kcal

Servings: 5

Ingredients:

- 4 cloves garlic, minced
- 1 tbsp. cooking oil
- 1 small yellow onion, thinly sliced
- 2 (14) oz. cans kidney beans, drained and rinsed
- A few fresh springs of cilantro
- 4 ½ cups of sweet potatoes, peeled and cut into 1/2" pieces
- 2 cups vegetable broth
- 1 ½ tbsp. chili powder
- ½ tsp. paprika
- 1/3 tsp. cayenne pepper
- 1 (15) oz. can minced tomatoes
- ¼ cup of bourbon
- 2 tbsp. maple syrup
- Salt and pepper, to taste
- 2 green onions, minced
- 3 small corn tortillas, toasted and sliced (optional)
- 2 tsp. cumin

Cooking Instructions:

1. Set your Instant Pot to sauté, put oil, and let it heat up for 40 seconds.

2. Add the onions and heat up for about 5 minutes, stir it periodically, until onions are fragrant. Put garlic and heat for another 40 seconds.

3. Add the shredded sweet potatoes, chili powder, cumin, paprika, and cayenne pepper, stir until vegetables are well coated.

4. Add the vegetable broth, beans, tomatoes, maple syrup, and bourbon. Close and lock the lid in place and ensure that the valve is in sealing position.

5. Select the Manual setting to cook on High Pressure for about 15 minutes. When the time is up, use a natural pressure release for about 12 minutes.

6. Carefully open the lid and check to make sure the sweet potatoes are tender.

7. If you are making use of tortillas, lightly oil a cast iron skillet and pan sauté the tortillas on each side for 3 minutes.

8. Carefully remove from heat and let cool before shredding into thin strips.

9. You may add these optional toppings: cilantro, green onions, and toasted tortillas.

10. Serve and enjoy!

Vegan Potato Curry

Preparation time: 12 minutes

Cooking time: 45 minutes

Total time: 57 minutes

Calories: 270 kcal

Servings: 5

Ingredients:

- 1 420ml can coconut milk, full fat or light
- 1 medium yellow onion, chopped
- 4 large cloves of garlic, chopped finely
- 950g and about 5 heaping cups baby potatoes
- 2 tbsp. curry powder or curry paste
- 500mls and around 2 cups water
- 3 tbsp. arrowroot powder.
- 1 tbsp. sugar
- Salt and pepper to taste
- 1 tsp. chili pepper flakes or a small fresh chili chopped
- 400g and 2 heaping cups fresh green beans, chopped into small sizes

Cooking Instructions:

1. Turn your Instant Pot to sauté mode. When hot, put a few drops of water and cook the onions until soft.

2. Add the garlic and cook for one minute. Press the keep warm/cancel button. Add everything else to the Instant Pot except the green beans and arrowroot.

3. Close and lock the lid in place and ensure that the valve is in sealing position. Press the manual key to cook on high pressure for about 20 minutes.

4. When the time is up, use a natural pressure release for about 16 minutes. Add the arrowroot into a small bowl and pour a few tablespoons of water to make it thick.

5. Pour it into the Instant Pot stirring continuously. Add salt and pepper to taste then add the green beans. Cook for about 5 minutes until they are soft and the gravy has thickened.

6. Serve immediately and enjoy!

APPETIZERS

Beer-Braised Pulled Ham

Preparation time: 15 minutes

Cooking time: 30 minutes

Total time: 45 minutes

Servings: 14

Ingredients:

- ½ tsp. coarsely ground pepper
- 2 bottles (12 oz. each) beer or nonalcoholic beer
- ¾ cup of German or Dijon mustard, divided
- 1 fully cooked bone-in ham (4 lb.)
- 16 pretzel hamburger buns, split
- Dill pickle slices (optional)
- 4 fresh rosemary sprigs

Cooking Instructions:

1. Whisk together beer, ½ cup of mustard and pepper into your Instant Pot.

2. Add the ham and rosemary. Close and lock the lid in place and ensure that the valve is in sealing position

3. Press the Manual key to cook on High Pressure for about 20 minutes. When the time is up, use a natural pressure release for about 15 minutes.

4. Carefully remove ham and allow it to cool. Discard rosemary sprigs. Skim fat from liquid remaining in Instant Pot.

5. Select sauté mode and set on high pressure. Boil your liquid for about 7 minutes.

6. Touch the ham. When it is cool enough to handle, cut meat with two forks.

7. Replace ham to Instant Pot; heat through.

8. Serve and enjoy!

Prosciutto-wrapped Asparagus Canes

Preparation time: 5 minutes

Cooking time: 7 minutes

Total time: 12 minutes

Servings: 5

Ingredients:

- 1 lb. (480g) thick Asparagus
- 8 oz. (235g) thinly sliced Prosciutto

Cooking Instructions:

1. Add small amount of water (1 to 2 cups) into your Instant Pot and keep aside.

2. Take the asparagus spears and wrap in prosciutto. Place any extra un-wrapped spears in a single layer on the bottom of the steamer basket to prevent the prosciutto from sticking.

3. Add the prosciutto-wrapped asparagus on top in a single layer also. Keep the basket inside the Instant pot.

4. Close and lock the lid in place and ensure that the valve is in sealing position. Press the Manual function to cook on High Pressure for about 3 minutes.

5. When the time is up, use a natural pressure release for about 5 minutes. Carefully open the lid once the pressure has been released.

6. Get the steamer basket out immediately and place the asparagus on a serving platter so they may not be gradually cooked by remaining heat.

7. Serve immediately and enjoy!

Buffalo Ranch Chicken Dip

Preparation time: 5 minutes

Cooking time: 20 minutes

Total time: 25 minutes

Calories: 506 kcal

Servings: 6

Ingredients:

- 1 ½ lb. chicken breast
- 1 packet ranch dip
- 1 ½ cup of Hot Sauce
- 1 stick butter
- 15 oz. cheddar cheese
- 8 oz. cream cheese

Cooking Instructions:

1. Add the chicken, cream cheese, butter, hot sauce, and a packet of ranch dip into the bottom of your Instant Pot.

2. Close and lock the lid in place and ensure that the valve is in sealing position.

3. Press the Manual key to cook on High Pressure for about 15 minutes.

4. When the time is up, use a natural pressure release for about 5 minutes.

5. Carefully open the lid once the pressure has been released.

6. Shred your chicken with fork or use your mixer to break it up and pour cheddar cheese.

7. Have some chips available.

8. Serve and enjoy!

Cocktail Meatballs

Preparation time: 5 minutes

Cooking time: 7 minutes

Total time: 12 minutes

Serves: 65 pieces

Ingredients:

- 1 tbsp. minced garlic
- 2 lb. cooked Perfect Homestyle Meatballs
- ¼ cup of honey
- ½ cup of ketchup
- 2 tbsp. soy sauce
- ⅓ cup of brown sugar
- Garnish with sliced green onions (optional)

Cooking Instructions:

1. Mix brown sugar, honey, ketchup, soy sauce, and garlic in pressure cooker.

2. Set to sauté mode and stir to mix properly.

3. When the mixture comes to a boil, put the frozen fully cooked meatballs.

4. Close and lock the lid in place and ensure that the valve is in sealing position.

5. Press the Manual function to cook on High Pressure for about 5 minutes.

6. When the time is up, use a natural pressure release for about 3 minutes.

7. Serve hot and enjoy!

Cranberry Pecan Brie

Preparation time: 15 minutes

Cooking time: 30 minutes

Total time: 45 minutes

Servings: 4

Ingredients:

- 1 (8-oz) round of Brie
- ¼ cup of cranberry jalapeno preserves
- 3 tbsp. candied pecans
- 1 tsp. minced fresh thyme

Cooking Instructions:

1. Slice through the rind on top of the Brie in a grid pattern.

2. Add the brie in a baking dish in a way it will fit in your instant pot and then cover baking dish tightly with foil.

3. Prepare a foil sling for lifting the baking dish out of the Instant Pot by taking an 18" strip of foil and folding it twice.

4. Pour 1 cup of water into the bottom of your Instant Pot and place the rack in the bottom.

5. Keep the baking dish on center of the foil strip and lower it into the instant pot on to the rack. Fold the foil strips down.

6. Close and lock the lid in place and ensure that the valve is in sealing position. Press the Manual setting to cook on High Pressure for about 20 minutes.

7. When the time is up, use a natural pressure release for about 10 minutes. Scoop to a serving plate and top with preserves, pecans and thyme.

8. Serve immediately and enjoy!

French Apple Cobbler

Preparation time: 25 minutes

Cook time: 35 minutes

Total time: 1 hour

Servings: 4-6 servings

Calories: 225 kcal

Ingredients:

Apple Mixture:

- 4 cups of sliced apples
- ½ cup of coconut sugar
- 2 tablespoons of gluten free flour
- ½ teaspoon of cinnamon
- ¼ teaspoon of nutmeg
- ½ teaspoon of sea salt
- 1 teaspoon of vanilla
- ¼ cup of water

Cobbler:

- ¾ cup of gluten free flour
- ¼ cup of coconut sugar
- 1 teaspoon of sea salt
- ½ teaspoon of baking powder
- ½ teaspoon of baking soda
- 4 ounces applesauce

Cooking Instructions:

1. In a medium bowl, mix together all Apple Mixture.

2. In another bowl, mix together all ingredients for Cobbler topping. Spoon cobbler mix on top of apple mixture.

3. Pour 1 cup of water into the bottom of your Instant Pot. Add the bowl on rack and place into Instant Pot.

4. Secure the lid in place and ensure that the valve is in sealing position. Select Manual High Pressure for 25 minutes.

5. Do a natural pressure release for about 10 minutes and carefully open the lid. Lift out the bowl from Instant Pot.

6. Place the bowl under broiler and broil for about 5 minutes or until your desired crisp is achieved.

7. Serve and enjoy!

Olive Garden Zuppa Toscana

Servings: 6

Preparation time: 15 minutes

Cook time: 20 minutes

Total time: 35 minutes

Ingredients:

- 1 tbsp. of olive oil
- 1 lb. mild Italian sausage, casing removed
- 3 cloves garlic, minced
- 1 onion, diced
- ½ tsp. of dried oregano
- 3 russet potatoes, chopped
- 6 cups of chicken broth
- Kosher salt and freshly ground black pepper, to taste
- ½ bunch kale, stems removed and leaves chopped
- 1 cup half and half

Cooking Instructions:

1. Set your Instant Pot to Sauté function and adjust to High.

2. Add the olive oil and sausage. Sauté, stirring frequently for about 4 minutes or until sausage is lightly browned. Drain the excess fat.

3. Add the garlic, onion and oregano. Cook, stirring frequently for about 2 minutes or until onions have turned translucent and soft.

4. Stir in potatoes and chicken broth; season with salt and pepper, to taste. Secure the lid in place and ensure that the valve is in sealing position.

5. Select Manual High Pressure for 5 minutes. Do a quick pressure release and carefully remove the lid.

6. Stir in kale until wilted for about 2 minutes. Stir in half and half until heated through, about 1 minute. Add salt and pepper, to taste.

7. Serve immediately and enjoy!

DESSERTS
Chocolate Pots De Crème

Servings: 6

Preparation time: 10 minutes

Cook time: 6 minutes

Total time: 16 minutes

Ingredients:

- 1 ½ cups of heavy cream
- ½ cup of whole milk
- 5 large egg yolks
- ¼ cup of sugar
- A pinch of salt
- 2 oz. bittersweet chocolate, melted
- Whipped cream and grated chocolate for decoration, optional

Cooking Instructions:

1. Bring the cream and milk to simmer in a small saucepan.

2. In a medium bowl, whisk together the egg yolks, sugar, and salt. Slowly whisk in the hot cream and milk.

3. Whisk in chocolate until blended. Add into 6 custard cups. Add 1 ½ cups of water into the bottom of your Instant Pot and place the trivet.

4. Add 3 cups on the trivet and insert another trivet on top of the cups. Place the remaining 3 cups on top of the second trivet.

5. Secure the lid in place and ensure that the valve is in sealing position. Select Manual High Press for 6 minutes.

6. Do a quick pressure release and carefully open the lid. Gently remove the cups to a wire rack to cool uncovered.

7. Refrigerate covered with plastic wrap for at least 4 hours or overnight.

8. Serve and enjoy!

Creamed Corn

Preparation time: 10 minutes

Cook time: 10 minutes

Total time: 20 minutes

Ingredients:

- 8 ounces Philadelphia cream cheese, cubed
- 1 stick unsalted butter, cut into pieces
- 3 15 ounces cans of organic whole kernel corn, drained
- 1 cup of milk
- 1 tablespoon of sugar
- ¼ teaspoon of black pepper
- ½ teaspoon of salt, or more to taste

Cooking Instructions:

1. Add the drained corn into the bottom of your Instant Pot.

2. Add the butter slices, cubed cream cheese, milk, and sugar.

3. Slowly give everything a good mix to combine. Secure lid in place

4. Select Low Pressure and set the timer for 10 minutes.

5. Do a natural pressure release, then quick release any remaining pressure.

6. Carefully open the lid and add salt and pepper to taste. Give everything a good stir.

7. Serve immediately and enjoy!

Chocolate Lava Cake

Preparation time: 10 minutes

Cook time: 12 minutes

Total time: 22 minutes

Servings: 4

Ingredients:

- 225 g self-rising flour
- 100 g butter
- 100 g caster sugar
- 30 g organic cocoa powder
- 100 g dark chocolate
- 2 eggs
- 30 ml whole milk
- 1 tablespoon of vanilla essence
- Handful fresh raspberries

Cooking Instructions:

1. In a medium bowl, add the butter and sugar and cream the fat into the sugar.

2. Beat in the eggs until it is well mixed. Add the milk, cocoa powder and vanilla and a little flour at a time until half of the flour is used.

3. Add squares of chocolate into the center of the mixture. Pour a cup of water into the bottom of your Instant Pot. Place the steamer rack inside the pot.

4. Add the bowl on the steamer rack. Secure the lid in place and ensure that the valve is in sealing position.

5. Select Steam function and set to cook for about 12 minutes. Do a quick pressure release when the timer beeps. Carefully open the lid.

6. Serve the chocolate pudding with fresh raspberries and enjoy!

Apple Crisp

Preparation time: 6 minutes

Cooking time: 8 minutes

Total time: 14 minutes

Servings: 5

Ingredients

- 2 ½ tsp. cinnamon
- ½ tsp. nutmeg
- ½ cup of water
- 1 tbsp. maple syrup
- 4 ½ tbsp. butter
- ¾ cup of old fashioned rolled oats
- ¼ cup of flour
- ¼ cup of brown sugar
- 5 medium sized apples, peeled and chopped into chunks ☐ ½ tsp. salt

Cooking Instructions:

1. Add the apples on the bottom of your Instant Pot.

2. Pour in cinnamon and nutmeg. Top with water and maple syrup.

3. Heat the butter to melt. Using a small bowl, mix together melted butter, oats, flour, brown sugar and salt. You can drop by the spoonful on top of the apples.

4. Close and lock the lid in place and ensure that the valve is in sealing position.

5. Press the Manual key to cook on High Pressure for about 10 minutes.

6. When the time is up, use a natural pressure release for about 8 minutes.

7. Add your toppings like vanilla ice cream.

8. Serve and enjoy!

Homemade Pumpkin Puree

Preparation time: 5 minutes

Cooking time: 14 minutes

Total time: 19 minutes

Servings: 5

Ingredients:

- 4 lbs. pie pumpkin
- 1 cup of water

Cooking Instructions

1. Remove the stem from the pumpkin.

2. Place a steamer basket in the bottom of the Instant Pot and put 1 cup of water.

3. Add the pumpkin on the basket cover the lid without touching the top of the pumpkin.

4. Close and lock the lid in place and ensure that the valve is in sealing position. Press the Manual key to cook on High Pressure for about 15 minutes.

5. When the time is up, use a natural pressure release for about 8 minutes. Carefully open the lid once the pressure has been released.

6. Remove the pumpkin from the Instant Pot (use the handles of the rack) and place on a cutting board. Allow it to cool until it is easy to handle.

7. Cut the pumpkin into half, remove the seeds, goop, and peel off the skin.

8. Using a regular blender, blend the soft pumpkin until smooth and add a tablespoon of water, if needed to help it along.

9. Serve and enjoy!

Gingerbread Bread Pudding

Preparation time: 10 minutes

Cook time: 20 minutes

Total time: 30 minutes

Servings: 6-8

Ingredients:

- 6 cups of cubed French bread
- 3 eggs
- 2 cups of milk
- 1/3 cup of brown sugar
- 2 tablespoons of molasses
- 1 teaspoon of vanilla extract
- 1 teaspoon of cinnamon
- 1 teaspoon of ginger (dried)
- ½ cup of chopped pecans
- 2 cups of water
- Almond butter, chocolate chips & pecans for topping, optional

Cooking Instructions:

1. In a medium bowl, combine together eggs, milk, brown sugar, molasses, cinnamon, ginger and chopped pecans and give everything a good mix.

2. Add the cubed bread and stir to coat. Allow it to sit for about 5 minutes. Transfer to a greased 1.5 quart glass bowl. Add a steamer rack in your Instant Pot.

3. Fold aluminum foil in half lengthwise and then in half again to make a sling. Add the bowl on the rack on top of the foil.

4. Pour 1.5 cups of water into the bottom of your Instant Pot. Secure the lid in place and ensure that the valve is in sealing position.

5. Select Manual High Pressure for 20 minutes. Do a quick pressure release and carefully open the lid. Remove the bowl from the pot using the foil sling.

6. Allow to rest and cool for about 5 minutes. Use a spatula or knife to trace around the edges and flip upside down to release onto a plate.

7. Drizzle on top along with extra chopped pecans. Serve topped with ice cream.

Applesauce

Preparation time: 3 minutes

Cooking time: 9 minutes

Total time: 12 minutes

Calories: 140 kcal

Servings: 5

Ingredients:

- 1 cup of water
- 2 drops cinnamon essential oil
- 1 tsp. organic cinnamon optional
- 7 mediums to large apples Granny Smith, Gala, McIntosh, Fuji, etc.

Cooking Instructions:

1. Slice apples into 2-inch chunks. Throw away the core, stem and seeds.
2. Add them in Instant Pot along with 1 cup of water.
3. Close and lock the lid in place and ensure that the valve is in sealing position.
4. Press the Manual button to cook on High Pressure for about 9 minutes.
5. When the time is up, use a natural pressure release for about 3 minutes.
6. Turn steam vent to release pressure. Carefully open the lid when all steam has evaporated.
7. Using immersion blender, blend to smooth out applesauce to your taste.
8. Add 2 drops of cinnamon oil or powder to taste. Allow it to cool or put in the refrigerator.
9. Serve and enjoy!

ACKNOWLEDGMENT

In preparing the **"The Instant Pot Cookbook"**, I sincerely wish to acknowledge my indebtedness to my wife Mrs. Clara Michael for her support and the wholehearted cooperation and vast experience of my two colleagues - Mrs. Jane Smith and Mrs. Nicole Fox.

Michael Francis

www.ingramcontent.com/pod-product-compliance
Lightning Source LLC
Chambersburg PA
CBHW081747100526
44592CB00015B/2331